Towards A Local Livelihood Security Framework

ABOUT THE AUTHORS

Harsh Singh has a rich cross-institutional background. He served in the Indian Economic Service for a decade and in UNDP India (1992 to 2009) as Assistant Resident Representative and Programme Advisor. He now heads the consultancy, Market Solutions for Inclusion. He has authored the books, *Creating Vibrant Public-Private-Panchayat Partnership* and *Structural Innovation for Inclusive Development in Bihar: The Navodaya Shahar Model*, both published by the Academic Foundation.

Vinayak Vishnu Damle, Senior Adviser (Water Management), Confederation of Indian Industry (CII), is a Civil Engineering graduate from Indian Institute of Technology (IIT) Bombay. He has been working on the issue of rural sustainable water management for over 15 years. He leads the CII Dungarpur Initiative, a pilot model for the development of backward districts.

Devilal Vyas is the Executive Director of the voluntary organisation Jan Shiksha Evam Vikas Sangathan (also known as People's Education and Development Organisation—PEDO). He has guided and supported the Government of Rajasthan, UNDP and various NGOs in their pro-poor policy and programme work.

Ramila Vyas is a co-founder of PEDO. She leads PEDO's activities in the areas of pro-poor livelihoods, women's empowerment and capacity building of PRI representatives.

Vishnu Bhagwat Khedkar is a Post Graduate in Agricultural Engineering and has worked for around a decade in the field of rural development with special focus on NRM-based livelihood. He was in-charge of the Dungarpur-based CII team that piloted the Public-Private-Community Partnership pilot in the district. He has also worked as a Co-Project Investigator for the Farmers Participatory Action Research Programme (FPARP) for demonstrating micro-irrigation techniques and efficient management of water resources for enhanced agricultural productivity.

Towards A Local Livelihood Security Framework

Evidence from Small and Marginal Women Farmers in Dungarpur

HARSH SINGH, VINAYAK VISHNU DAMLE,
DEVILAL VYAS, RAMILA VYAS AND
VISHNU BHAGWAT KHEDKAR

ACADEMIC FOUNDATION
NEW DELHI

www.academicfoundation.com

First published in 2013
by

ACADEMIC FOUNDATION
4772-73 / 23 Bharat Ram Road, (23 Ansari Road),
Darya Ganj, New Delhi - 110 002 (India).
Phones : 23245001 / 02 / 03 / 04.
Fax : +91-11-23245005.
E-mail : books@academicfoundation.com
www.academicfoundation.com

Cataloging in Publication Data--DK

Courtesy: D.K. Agencies (P) Ltd. <docinfo@dkagencies.com>

Towards a local livelihood security framework : evidence from small and marginal women farmers in Dungarpur / Harsh Singh ... [et al.].
p. Cm.
Includes bibliographical references (p.).
ISBN 9789332700154

1. Women farmers--India--Dungarpur--Economic conditions. 2. Farms, Small--India--Dungarpur. 3. Agriculture--Economic aspects--India--Dungarpur. 4. Rural poor--Government policy--India--Dungarpur. I. Singh, Harsh.

DDC 338.108209544 23

Typeset by Italics India, New Delhi.

Printed and bound by The Book Mint, New Delhi.
www.thebookmint.in.

Contents

List of Tables, Figures and Boxes *7*

Preface *11*

1. **Introduction** **15**

Unravelling the Paradox of Poverty in Backward Districts

Towards a Local Livelihood Security Framework: The Context of the Study and Overview of Results

The Chapterisation Scheme

2. **The Rural Livelihood Baseline** **25**

The State of Agriculture and Livelihoods

Feminisation of Agriculture

The Rural Baseline in India and Rural-Urban Linkages

Rural Livelihood and Rural Governance

3. **The Women and NRM Survey in Dungarpur: Sample Characteristics and Survey Methodology** **39**

Sample Villages

The Sample Population

Survey Design and Methodology

4. **Results of the Women and NRM Survey in Dungarpur** **45**

Women Farmers are not Residual or Workers by Default

Empowerment

Priorities in Decision-Making

Women Farmers and Credit

Knowledge and Capacity Building Needs

Benefits from Laws, Policies and Government Programmes

Evidence on Social Capital and its Far Reaching Implications

Conclusion

5. **The Perspective of Women PRI Leaders 75**

Introduction

Women as Farmers

Perception on Government Policies and Programmes

Functioning of PRIs

Women Leadership

Creation of a Community-based Extension Support System

Results of the Focus Group Discussions in Village Nimsariya, Hoshangabad District, Madhya Pradesh

Conclusion

6. **The Backward Regions Grant Fund (BRGF): Community Response Towards a Redesign.................. 89**

Overview of BRGF

World Bank Assessment of BRGF

The BRGF Plan for Dungarpur (2011-12)

Community Response Towards a Redesign of BRGF

7. **Towards a Local Livelihood Security Framework for Inclusive Development and Inclusive Governance........... 97**

Introduction

Locally-owned Extension Mechanism for Small and Marginal Farmers

Refocusing Decentralisation Towards a Locally-owned and Locally-driven Livelihood Security Framework

Annexures 113

References 131

List of Tables, Figures and Boxes

Tables

1.1 Women Farmers: Do the Following Recognise Your Efforts and Contribution as a Farmer? . . . 16

2.1 District-wise Distribution of Household Requiring Services from Various Institutions . . . 35

2.2 Caste-wise Distribution of Households Requiring Services of Various Institutions . . . 36

2.3 Approachability of Panchayats: Caste–wise Distribution of Respondents . . . 36

2.4 Community Perception on the Role of Institutions . . . 37

3.1 Socioeconomic Profile of Selected Sample Villages . . . 41

3.2 Profile of Respondents . . . 43

3.3 Pattern of Land Ownership in the Sample Population . . . 43

4.1 Women Farmers: Likely Impact of an Increase in Income from Other Sources on their Farming Efforts . . . 45

4.2 Will Women Farmers Shift to an Urban Area if their Spouse/Other Members of the Household Found Well Paid Employment There? . . . 46

4.3 Choice of Vocation for Educated Daughters . . . 46

4.4 Details of Work Distribution between Women Farmers and Other Members . . . 47

4.5 Details of Other Incomes . . . 48

4.6 Control over the Use of Income Earned . . . 48

4.7 Participation in Decision-Making . . . 49

4.8 Recognition of Efforts and Contribution as a Farmer . . . 50

4.9 Women Farmers: Results of Recognition of their Efforts and Contribution as a Farmer 50

4.10 Results of Lack of Recognition of Efforts and Contribution as a Farmer. 51

4.11 Land Title and Empowerment of Women Farmers 52

4.12 Considerations by Women Farmers While Planning Farming Activities 53

4.13 Do You Think that Your Spouse's Response to Planning Farming Activities will be Different from Yours?. 54

4.14 Perception of Women Farmers Regarding the Considerations Important to their Spouse in Planning Farming Activities 54

4.15 Frequency of Loans by Women Farmers in the Last Three Years. 55

4.16 Credit Source of Choice 55

4.17 Who Takes the Decision Regarding Credit? 56

4.18 Activities for which Women Farmers Took Credit 56

4.19 Credit and Building Sustainable Income Assets 57

4.20 Self-Perception about Knowledge to Derive Maximum Output from Farming 58

4.21 Self-Perception about Awareness with Regard to Various Agricultural Practices. 58

4.22 Measures Outlined by Women Farmers for Supporting them in Improving Farm Output 59

4.23 Training Needs. 60

4.24 Irrigation Practices 62

4.25 Mechanisation Needed to Reduce Burden and Drudgery for Women Farmers 62

4.26 If Mechanisation Service is Made Available in the Village, Would You Like to Take Benefit of it by Paying Competitive Services Charges?. 63

4.27 Are Laws and Policies Supporting Women Farmers? 63

4.28 Benefits Derived from Government Schemes. 64

4.29 Benefits from NREGS 66

4.30 Participation in Gram Sabha 67

4.31 Responses on the Main Role of *Panchayats* 67

4.32 Committees Existing in the Village 68

4.33 Do Women Farmers Need to Come Together to Create a Support Structure/SHG to Get Suitable Services of Agriculture Experts, Animal Doctor, Credit Facilitator etc.? 69

4.34 Three Most Important Needs that a Local Group Could Help Meet 69

4.35 Level at which the Group Needs to be Formed to Serve Best the Local Interest while Keeping Costs Manageable 70

4.36 Response on Willingness to Contribute for Creating and Maintaining the Local Group 70

4.37 Who should Set Up the Support Structure? 71

4.38 Will Greater Role for Leadership by Women Improve Development? 72

4.39 Response on Positive Aspects of Womens' Leadership 72

4.40 What are the Qualities that You Would Like to See in Women Leaders? 73

4.41 Identify Priorities that You would Like Women Leader to Address? 74

6.1 Block-wise Allocations Approved in the BRGF Plan for Dungarpur for 2011-12 93

7.1 Expenditure on Flagship Development Programmes over the Eleventh Plan 98

Figures

5.1 Schematic Presentation of Natural Resource Management 85

7.1 Technical Consortium 105

Boxes

1.1 Why Farmers are not Accessing Information? 21

2.1 Agri-Extension Services in India: Need for a Paradigm Shift 28

3.1 Dungarpur District: An Overview 40

7.1 CII's Half-Hectare Model: PPCP Strategy 100

7.2 Empowering Local Communities to 'Produce Locally-Consume Locally' (A Contribution to the e-Discussion on the UN Food and Nutrition Community of Practice) 109

Preface

This modest study has evolved considerably. This is on account of the striking findings from a survey of women farmers carried out in Dungarpur, Rajasthan as a part of this study, but also the developments of far reaching significance in the economic environment as well as the churning in the public space on issues such as the Food Security Bill, the poverty line and particularly around the themes of public accountability and participation.

It became clear that the voices from the small and marginal women farmers captured in the village survey in the remote tribal-dominated Dungarpur district had a direct bearing on the weighty deliberations in the Yojana Bhawan, the Supreme Court, the Ramlila Maidan and Jantar Mantar in far away Delhi. Thus, this report consciously moves away from a technical discussion of the proximate issues of women in agriculture to linking the broader strands of public policy standing at the crossroads with the grassroot reality.

The Report concludes that the buoyancy in the Indian economy over the past decade has had a serious unforeseen consequence. The rising revenue base of the Central government in the face of growing political competition as defined by a mosaic of different political parties capturing power in some key states has resulted in a pre-occupation with grand centrally-driven social security programmes. Paradoxically, the decentralisation momentum which is the natural route to achieving social objectives appears to be getting lost in this game of large sums.

The pursuit of such centrally-driven grandiose strategy is putting tremendous pressure on the fiscal balance that threatens to undermine the economic base of the new resurgent India. This approach is pitting the social objectives against the economic objectives. This trend needs to be corrected as the two cannot survive and prosper without a symbiotic relationship.

The answer to the fast deteriorating economic baseline in the closing years of the Eleventh Plan and the current social churning lies in creating manageable, locally-relevant and locally-driven livelihood compact rather than in the grandiose centrally-driven programmes that seek to address different strands of social security in isolation or in the artificial attempts at top-down convergence between such initiatives.

The unique value of this modest study is in generating firm evidence to show that the populace even in a remote and backward district stands ready to embrace such a livelihood compact and spurns alternatives that smack of charity.

Fortunately, the year 2011 has been quite richly endowed with publications on women in development from major international agencies such as the World Bank, the Food and Agricultural Organization of the UN (FAO), the International Fund for Agriculture Development (IFAD) and the World Economic Forum (WEF). Thus, those interested in the details of the women in agriculture theme would do well to refer to these or to numerous outstanding contributions in this area from national sources.

I take this opportunity to thank Rita Sarin, Country Director of the Hunger Project, Dharampreet Singh, Advisor and Sourabh Ghosh, Programme Officer for reposing faith in this follow-up study and for extending excellent cooperation and support. I thank Dr Renana Jahabwala, Chairperson SEWA Bharat and Dr Sanjay Kumar, Director for providing a platform for conducting this study. I thank Anita Sajwan and Needhi of this organisation for providing excellent implementation support.

Lastly, this study is the result of excellent partnership with the Confederation of Indian Industry (CII) team working on the Dungarpur Public-Private-Community Partnership (PPCP) Project and with the Jan Siksha Evam Vikas Sangathan of Dungarpur popularly known as PEDO or People's Education and Development Organisation. The CII team was led by Vinayak Damle, Senior Advisor (and a well known expert in water management), Vishnu Khedkar and Hari Mohan who are specialists in agriculture. Vishnu assumed ownership of the survey in Dungarpur and saw it through successfully. The PEDO team was led by Devi Lal Vyas and Ramilla Vyas. These two highly respected social leaders have dedicated their entire life to the cause of the tribal population in Dungarpur. Ramilla ji personally led various focus group discussions and oversaw the survey in which the PEDO team played a crucial role. This ensured quality assurance of the highest order. I also thank Amitabh Singh and Leena Singh of the Madhya Pradesh-based NGO, Debate for agreeing to organise some focus group meetings locally as a quality control measure for the findings in Dungarpur.

On behalf of the team that executed this study, I express the hope that this crucial set of evidence from the small and marginal farmers in Dungarpur will contribute to the ongoing churning on a workable pro-poor development model.

— Harsh Singh
Project Coordinator and Director,
Market Solutions to Inclusion

1 Introduction

Unravelling the Paradox of Poverty in Backward Districts

'India grapples with the paradox of endemic backwardness in over 250 districts while certain sections and sectors are moving at a pace that is making global headlines,' noted the report, "Creating Vibrant Public-Private-Panchayat Partnership (PPPP) for Inclusive Growth through Inclusive Governance" prepared under the aegis of the National Platform for Promoting Decentralisation (Singh, 2010). This follow-up study, "Towards a Local Livelihood Security Framework", brings-up powerful evidence on the nature of this paradox.

The evidence emerges from a survey of 190 women farmers across eight villages in the backward district of Dungarpur in Rajasthan. This sample population comprising predominantly below poverty line (BPL) families from the scheduled tribe (ST) community residing in one of the most backward districts in India shows remarkable dynamism. Their response presents a message that is of considerable importance for both inclusive growth strategies and inclusive governance models.

Knowledge input emerges as the top most priority of the women farmers surveyed. They prefer assured irrigation facility over monetary subsidy from the government. They are highly enthusiastic about the prospects of coming together to create a local support structure for agri-extension services. Also, despite their extremely meagre resource base, they responded with a resounding 'yes' to contributing in cash for support services that generate long-term benefits.

But such innate dynamism at the grassroots is seldom noticed or nurtured, and this stakeholder group capable of leading the transformation process is clubbed into an omnibus category of 'the poor'. The paradox referred to above lies in this hiatus between the potential and the ground reality.

Table 1.1

Women Farmers: Do the Following Recognise Your Efforts and Contribution as a Farmer?

Categories	*Yes, Adequately*	*Yes, But Not Fully*	*Do Not Recognise*
Your spouse	98	20	16
Other members of the household	125	10	1
Other women farmers in the neighborhood	120	10	6
Community leaders	58	30	48
Panchayat members	8	47	77
Local NGOs	11	42	81
Government functionaries at local level e.g. *gram sewak*	15	26	90
Government functionaries at higher level e.g. collector	4	18	111
Political leaders e.g. the MLA	2	9	111

The evidence emerging from this modest survey in Dungarpur has tremendous significance for the current debate on strategies for poverty alleviation, social security and growth in the context of a fast deteriorating international economic environment, unabated domestic inflation, rising fiscal deficit and a dip in the overall growth rates.

The Eleventh Plan with its focus on 'faster and more inclusive growth' targeted a decline in the poverty ratio by 2 percentage points per year. But preliminary estimates using the NSS survey for 2009 suggest a slippage of 50 per cent *vis-à-vis* the above target (during the five-year period—2004-05 to 2009-10) despite an expenditure of ₹ 691,976 crore across 13 programmes aimed at building rural and urban infrastructure (see Chapter 7, Table 7.1). Thus, the conclusion of the Twelfth Plan Approach Paper that while the result with regard to poverty alleviation was below the target, it was actually better than in the earlier decade (i.e., 0.8 percentage points per year during 1993-94 to 2004-05) is not acceptable to most. This is also clear from the public outcry over the Planning Commission's position on the poverty line in its affidavit to the Supreme Court in September 2011.

Increasingly the entire approach to poverty estimation, identification, targetting etc., is being brought to question.

The goal of universal social security and safety net underlying recent initiatives such as the Mahatma Gandhi National Rural Employment Guarantee Scheme (MGNREGS), the Right to Education, the Forest Rights Act and the Food Security Bill is unquestionable to most. However, there is considerable difference of opinion with regard to the strategies for realising such rights. By their very nature, these rights require local empowerment and local solutions. But, the buoyancy in the Indian economy over the past decade has led to a thaw in the decentralisation momentum. The goal of genuine decentralisation has given way to instruments such as 'convergence' of various centrally-driven initiatives and reliance on programmes such as the Backward Regions Grant Fund (BRGF) which provides a paltry sum of ₹ 20 crore per annum to each backward district as discretionary expenditure or similar special programmes for the extremist-ridden areas. The Twelfth Plan Approach Paper continues in a similar vein.

The sharp downturn in 2011 forewarns against the perils of papering over structural issues by flashing large sums of money. It is a timely reminder for reviving and resurrecting a genuine initiative in the area of decentralisation and building the blocks of a local livelihood security framework. Many of the state governments are taking initiatives towards implementation of the modality of citizen charters. States such as Madhya Pradesh, Bihar, Jammu and Kashmir, Punjab, Delhi, Rajasthan and Goa have in recent times taken strides in the direction of Public Service Guarantee Acts (UN Solution Exchange, 2011a). Such measures towards recognising the rights of citizens, timely and efficient delivery of services, enhancing transparency in service provision, holding service providers accountable and bringing citizens closer to the government are a step in the right direction. However, such rights-based instruments will achieve their transformational potential only when they are aligned to a wholesome developmental compact aimed at boosting the local livelihood baseline rather than to some discrete points of government-citizen interface.

The evidence from this modest survey of small and marginal women farmers in Dungarpur promises a ready ground for a giant leap in inclusive development and inclusive governance.

Towards a Local Livelihood Security Framework: The Context of the Study and Overview of Results

The PPPP report (Singh, 2010) concluded that poverty has become endemic in about 250 districts in India because of a combination of factors:

- An all pervasive weakness in the public agricultural extension machinery that is stunting both local productivity and value addition opportunities.
- Narrow and lop-sided vision of *panchayat*-level leaders, especially in so far as their role in agriculture is concerned.
- Lack of an organised PPP framework resulting in limited spread of benefits from the capacities and networks that a number of business agencies have built up.
- Weak community capacity, and gender and social inequities.
- Overall, a near monopoly by government agencies in public development efforts and in the use of public resources and assets.

The PPPP report articulated the need for a robust framework for local governance and development that could empower local leadership and initiative on the one hand, and pave the way for modern enterprises to unleash their technical, managerial and institutional capacity in the rural livelihoods chain on the other.

Showcasing an action research project of the Confederation of Indian Industry (CII) in Dungarpur that pointed to the possibility of ensuring to each tribal family, an income of over ₹ 25,000 per annum on 0.5 hectare plots in a challenging eco-environment, the PPPP report argued the case for a rural service enterprise framework. It noted that this concept was already operational in its various mutations, but on a micro-scale, and called for an organised and broad-based effort in this direction that includes key public initiatives and programmes such as the BRGF (Singh, 2010).

This study, "Towards a Local Livelihood Security Framework" supported by The Hunger Project takes forward the above development discussion. At the core of this study is a survey of small and marginal women farmers across eight villages in Dungarpur in order to explore the baseline of multiple vulnerabilities that this stakeholder group faces, to identify areas of strength and opportunities and to delineate the implications for inclusive growth strategies and inclusive governance models. The Term of Reference (ToR) of the study may be seen at Annexure A-1.

The survey covered 190 women farmers across eight villages in the Dungarpur district. Women farmers from the ST community comprised about 93 per cent of the sample population. Eighty-two per cent of the respondents belonged to the BPL category and another 5 per cent were from the Antodaya category. Over 90 per cent of the respondents had participated in MGNREGS. Six out of the eight sample villages fall in the category of dry land farming in a highly fragile economic environment. Thus, this sample unambiguously represents a sub-section of the population that is at the core of India's inclusive growth concerns.

The survey results are highly insightful. They first of all, dispel the notion that women farmers are 'residual workers' or that they work on farms by default because of the absence of other opportunities. About two-third of the women farmers surveyed indicated that their efforts in farming, instead of going down will receive a boost due to increased availability of resources, if the spouse/other members of the household earned enough from other sources to take care of the family needs. Similarly, nearly three-fourths of the respondents indicated that they would not like to move to urban areas even if the spouse found a well paid employment there.

This feedback flags a caveat to the findings emerging from the NSSO's *Situation Assessment Survey* in 2003 according to which 40 per cent of the farmers did not like farming, mainly for the reason that it was not profitable. Such an orientation, especially in the context of a stakeholder group facing multiple vulnerabilities calls for deeper analysis into the changing balance of factors impacting the livelihoods of the so- called poor. The results of this women and natural resource management (NRM) survey provide a glimpse into these realities.

The survey shows a sense of progress in education and health services, although the baseline continues to be highly sub-optimal. MGNREGS receives high rating with regard to its contribution to improved food security of the family and in checking migration of family members. The availability of agricultural inputs and knowledge on agriculture also receive high rating. But as further evidence outlined in Chapter 5 shows, this finding needs to be interpreted carefully.

On the other hand, the rating on progress in availability of water, fodder and forest—factors critical for rural livelihoods—is quite low. Similarly, MGNREGS which receives positive scores on a number of aspects, receives a low score with regard to transparency in the use of funds and medium scores in so far as creation of village-level assets is concerned.

The response to the question, 'Do you think laws and governement policies are supporting women's role as a farmer?' is largely in affirmative. But as is clear from the responses presented in Table 1.1, and the feedback from women PRI leaders presented in Chapter 5, an altogether different picture emerges in so far as the unfolding of the policies at the ground level is concerned.

The 'road ahead' emerging from this survey may come as a surprise to many as it departs radically from the popular notion on the needs of the poor and the marginalised communities.

The response to the question, 'What measures are required to support you in improving farm output?' shows that women farmers attach highest priority to various aspects relating to acquisition of knowledge and capacity building. This goes against the grain of popular understanding that has resulted in proliferation of subsidy-oriented programmes which rarely reach the poor communities. It is also important to note in this context that training programmes funded by the government covered not more than a quarter of the women farmers participating in the survey.

As per the survey, while ensuring suitable availability of food and fodder emerges as the overwhelming priority in this resource poor and fragile eco-environment, ensuring best possible returns from farming is also high in the priority list of women farmers. The responses in favour of maximising returns were four times higher than the response for minimizing risks and containing input costs.

Also, the women farmers surveyed showed preference for assured irrigation facility over monetary help from the government. Despite a meagre resource base, they unequivocally affirmed their willingness to pay for services considered to be in their long-term interest. Thus, the profile of decision variables that emerges from this study points to a highly modern and informed decision-making approach.

The response pattern also shows a high propensity for local cooperation in terms of sharing of equipment, water resources, as well as labour. There was an overwhelming affirmative response to the question on the need for women farmers to come togather to create a local extension mechanism.

Thus, the survey results provide new insights into issues such as the limited spread of agri-extension services that continue to puzzle scholars and policy makers.

Box 1.1

Why Farmers are not Accessing Information?

Despite the variety of agricultural extension approaches that operate in parallel and sometimes duplicate one another, the majority of farmers in India do not have access to any source of information. This severely limits their ability to increase their productivity and income and thereby reduce poverty. The importance of improving the coverage and relevance of agricultural extension in India therefore cannot be underestimated. Research to understand why farmers are not accessing information will be useful in designing an extension system that adequately caters to the information needs of farmers in rainfed and irrigated regions, in different agro-climatic zones, with various sizes of landholdings, and of both genders. Understanding the behavior of farmers in seeking information for their enterprises and communication through social networks will assist in the development of appropriate agricultural extension strategies. The existence of context-specific and relevant information for farmers also needs to be considered.

Source: Glendenning *et al.* (2010).

It is clear that instead of being passive recipients of public-welfare measures delivered through a bewildering array of programmes, this stakeholder group needs to be in the forefront of development. The former approach not only wastes precious resources, there is a much more serious danger of blunting and misdirecting developmental impulses at the community level. This book advances the case for transforming development support through new compact-oriented mechanisms that boost the community capacity for self-help.

Similarly, the lessons for inclusive governance models are clear. The survey results show that the community accords a lower priority to the traditional functions of PRIs such as resolving local disputes in favour of a direct role for them in the livelihoods arena.

Overall, this modest survey of small and marginal farmers in Dungarpur provides clinching evidence in favour of an approach grounded on local livelihood security framework.

The Chapterisation Scheme

Chapter 2 presents an overview of the rural livelihoods baseline as a context for interpreting the results of this study. The "State of India's Livelihoods: The 4P Report" produced by Access Development Services (Datta and Sharma, 2010) sums up the baseline. It concludes, '...several indicators of the economic health of farming and farmers have significantly improved over the years...yet livelihood deficit as indicated by statistics on incomes, expenditure, indebtedness and poverty described earlier continues to be large, particularly among the marginal holders, the landless and agricultural labourers' (Papola, 2010).

The Mahila Kisan Sashaktikaran Pariyojana (MKSP, 2011) focusing on gender inequity in agriculture states,

> ...agriculture, the single largest production endeavour in India, contributing to 16 per cent of the GDP is increasingly becoming a female activity... agriculture sector employs 80 per cent of all economically active women... (yet) women in agriculture are generally not able to access extension services and production assets like seed, water, credit, subsidy etc. As most of them are not recognized as farmers for want of ownership of land, they are not considered as beneficiaries of various government programmes/ services.

Chapter 2 also outlines the conclusions of a recent study by Krishna and Bajpai (2011) on rural-urban linkages and their impact on the rural baseline in India. The study concludes, 'the distribution of benefits from economic growth since the early 1990s has followed an identifiable spatial pattern. People in the largest cities have achieved the greatest gains, followed by people in small towns and villages close to towns. Further away, in villages located more than five kilometres from the nearest town—home to more than half of the entire population of India—inflation-adjusted per capita incomes fell between 1993 and 2005. The steepest declines were experienced by the lowest income groups. Rising inequality is a natural result of these spatially distributed trends. The debilitating effects of "distance from town" need to be countered by connecting outlying villages with more and better physical and social infrastructures.'

Chapter 2 presents evidence to show that *panchayati raj* has grown a strong local base. Thus, instead of looking up for devolution, it needs to draw on its local base to create a robust local livelihood security framework. It is the only institution that has the mandate and the potential to do so.

Chapter 3 presents the sample characteristics. It is clear that the sample population unambiguously represents a stakeholder group that is at the core of India's inclusive growth agenda. This chapter also provides an overview of the survey methodology and its limitations.

Chapter 4 presents the results of the Dungarpur Survey. The survey throws light on the division of labour between women and men. It delves into different aspects of empowerment such as control over the use of income from various sources and recognition of roles by different stakeholders. It explores the baseline in terms of the existing capacity as well as the capacity building needs of women farmers. By consciously including the softer aspects of capacity building, the survey brings to light issues that usually remain ignored in the context of discourses on poverty alleviation. Equally, the survey explores various aspects of social capital.

An overview of the survey result has been provided above. Overall, even in the context of a hostile eco-environment, a consistent picture of tremendous dynamism at the grassroot level, emerges. The survey also provides a rich feedback on what is working at the ground level and what is not? But most important, the survey results help delineate a clear way forward.

Chapter 5 outlines the result of a focus group meeting with a dozen PRI members organised to validate the survey findings, and particularly to gain perspective on the way forward. The women PRI leaders articulated a clear set of priorities: year-round availability of clean drinking water, quality education in villages, work towards resolving issues relating to agriculture with major focus on availability of irrigation to all and supply of quality agri-inputs. They unanimously cited another priority area. This was to discuss thoroughly in *panchayat* general meetings, every activity/scheme proposed to be implemented in the village and to incorporate without any bias genuine issues relating to village development.

The women PRI leaders also articulated in some depth, the contours of a local extension and support mechanism. It is clear that they accord high priority to participation, local ownership and control.

Chapter 6 outlines the views of women PRI members on re-organisation of BRGF which is a discretionary window of ₹ 20 crore allocated annually to PRIs in each backward district for meeting their unique local needs not covered under other programmes. It is shocking that not a single women PRI leader participating in the focus group had heard about BRGF which is cited in policy documents as a flagship initiative. The agenda suggested by these local leaders for BRGF brings out the clarity of their vision.

Chapter 7 sums up the conclusions and policy lessons emerging from this study. It outlines the contours of the CII's half-hectare PPCP model designed to ensure to each tribal family, an income of over ₹ 25,000 per annum on 0.5 hectare plots even under a challenging eco-environment. This shows the power and potential of local compacts in tackling backwardness.

Chapter 8 also flags the dangers of a slackening in the decentralisation momentum as a result of the upsurge in the economy over the Tenth and the Eleventh Plan. It warns of the perils of mounting large efforts towards the goal of universal social security without creating a strong local foundation. The latter is a necessary condition for harnessing local initiative and for creating strategies molded to the local reality. It concludes that the evidence from this modest survey of small and marginal women farmers in Dungarpur promises a ready ground for a giant leap in inclusive development and inclusive governance following the concept of local livelihood security framework.

2 The Rural Livelihood Baseline

The State of Agriculture and Livelihoods

This chapter attempts to define the rural livelihood baseline so as to set the context for the findings of the Dungarpur Survey and the recommendations based on it.

In India, although agriculture now contributes only about 17 per cent to GDP, it continues to employ about 55 per cent of the workforce. Papola (2010) states,

> ... at all India level, more than 80 per cent of the farmers belong to marginal and small farm size groups, owning or operating less than 2 hectares of land. The percentage of marginal and small farmers in the total, and also the land operated by them has steadily increased over time. The percentage of marginal farmers has gone up from nearly 38 per cent in 1953-54 to about 70 per cent in 2002-03. As per the Farmer's Survey, 54 per cent income is from wage income and only 26 per cent is from cultivation among the marginal farmer households (owning less than 1 ha of land). The share of income from animal farming (5.5 per cent) is also the highest for this category of farmers. Among small farmers, 56 per cent of the income is from cultivation while 30 per cent is from wages (NCEUS, 2009: 247).

The National Commission on Farmers (2006) chaired by M.S. Swaminathan noted that the average farm size had become smaller and the cost-risk-return structure of farming had become adverse. The Commission called for the development and introduction of a 'livelihood security package' for farmers by providing them technology choice according to agro-ecological conditions and market demand, soil health enhancement and water conservation, quality and affordability of inputs, credit and insurance and market tie-up, besides necessary health care facilities linked with the National Rural Health Mission (NRHM). It called for a strategy for achieving a four per cent growth rate in agriculture through the above package. Considering the importance of livestock in the rural economy, the Commission underlined the need to establish a Livestock Feed and Fodder Corporation. The Commission also drew attention to the need for diversifying sustainable livelihood opportunities on the lines of the Chinese model of township and village enterprises (TVEs). Towards this, it called for a 'Rural Non-Farm Livelihood Initiative' in form of agri-business centres, food parks and other rural non-farm employment programmes by restructuring agencies such as the Khadi and Village Industries Commission (KVIC).

The Commission noted, 'so far there has been no well defined policy for farmers. When finalised and adopted, the NCF-initiated National Policy for Farmers will be the first of its kind in the 10,000 years history of Indian farming.' The Commission detailed a Draft Mission Statement for Farmers calling for mainstreaming the human dimension in all farm policies and giving explicit attention to issues relating to agriculture.

Although the Commission report[1] was not implemented in totality, it influenced the national policy. Papola (2010) notes,

> The farm sector needs special attention not only in terms of growth in output but also for ensuring sustenance and improvement in the livelihoods of those engaged in agriculture has always been recognized, but it seems to have been taken up as a special challenge by the government in recent years.

Besides enhancing the growth target in the agricultural sector from 3 per cent per annum to 4 per cent per annum, the Eleventh Plan highlighted the need for a suitable strategy with regard to 85 per cent of the farmers who are small and marginal, increasingly female, and who find it difficult to access inputs, credit and extension or to market their output (Planning Commission[2]). The Plan called for a regionally differentiated strategy, particularly in respect of rainfed areas. The National Agricultural Development Programme (NADP) or the Rashtriya Krishi Vikas Yojana (RKVY) launched in 2007 seeks to decentralise the planning of agricultural development at the state and district levels keeping in view

---

1. Government of India, Ministry of Agriculture (*http://agricoop.nic.in/NCF/Revised%20Draft%20NPF%20of%20NCF.pdf*)
2. Government of India, Planning Commission (*http://planningcommission.nic.in/plans/planrel/fiveyr/welcome.html*)

the agro-climatic conditions, natural resource endowments and local needs. Similarly, the Macro Management of Agriculture Scheme (MMAS) has a special focus on the development of degraded land and soils and seeks to encourage the states to align programmes to regional conditions and priorities.

Limited penetration of agricultural extension services despite the significant dependence of the rural economy on agriculture continues to be an area of considerable concern. A Planning Commission (2007) Working Group Report observed, 'agricultural extension by government is almost non-existent at village level because government has less staff and its focus is mainly on subsidy schemes...'

While public extension services in the agricultural sector have not kept pace with the new challenges and opportunities, a number of business agencies have built up impressive capacities and networks in input supply and extension services. However, their outreach is yet quite small and confined mostly to agriculturally advanced regions.

Thus, the results of policy measures have been mixed. The "State of India's Livelihoods: The 4P Report" (Datta and Sharma, 2010) concludes,

> Strategies and policies relating to agriculture have focused on both the aspects—growth and special benefits to disadvantaged groups—to varying extent at different periods of time and, of course, to the varying and generally only moderate extent of success...several indicators of the economic health of farming and farmers have significantly improved over the years...yet livelihood deficit as indicated by statistics on incomes, expenditure, indebtedness and poverty described earlier continues to be large, particularly among the marginal holders, the landless and agricultural labourers. There is also a very clear regional dimension of the livelihood problem, based on agro-climatic characteristics of states and areas. In general, states with dominance of rainfed farming have much poorer, more vulnerable livelihoods among their farmers than those with major part of their farming receiving assured irrigation. There are, of course, special factors in hilly and tribal areas which restrict improvements in the incomes and livelihoods of their farmers (Papola, 2010).

Box 2.1

Agri-Extension Services in India: Need for a Paradigm Shift

Despite the renewed interest and investment in agricultural extension in India, the coverage of such services is inadequate. Government extension programmes, extension services of the national agricultural research system, cooperatives and non-governmental extension programmes have a very limited outreach (NSSO, 2005). The 2003 NSSO survey showed that 60 per cent of farmers had not accessed any source of information on modern technology to assist in their farming practices in the past year. Of those who had sourced information, 16 per cent received it from other progressive farmers, followed by input dealers. Of those farmers who had accessed information, the major problem of extension services was found to be the practical relevance of the advice (NSSO, 2005). The coverage and relevance of information provided to farmers through the agricultural extension system is therefore questionable. While this may be partly due to inadequate contact by the services, which need to reach a large and complex farming community, inappropriate or poor-quality information could also be a key hindrance to farmers' use of extension services. In other words, the content of the information provided by agricultural extension approaches, and the information farmers actually need, may not be aligned.

If extension is to remain relevant in India, particularly for marginal and smallholder farmers in rainfed regions, it needs to evolve to provide a diverse set of services that support agricultural livelihoods, offering relevant technologies that are integrated with appropriate services. Agricultural extension should also support and address relevant areas beyond the farm, such as storage, processing, market access and trade, agri-business management and entrepreneurship, natural resource management, and issues related to women. Within the paradigm of innovation systems, extension agencies can act as innovation intermediaries or innovation brokers, working with many partners to strengthen linkages and provide support for innovations. There must be innovations in extension delivery that embrace different methods and offer flexible adaptations to cater to the needs of users across states, regions, and communities. Extension must be able to respond to emerging issues in agriculture. Content needs to be part of an integrated knowledge system in which all actors in the food and agriculture value chain collaborate, contribute knowledge, and share the knowledge among the users.

Source: Glendenning *et al.* (2010).

Feminisation of Agriculture

The Planning Commission (2007) noted,

> About 85 per cent of rural female workers are working in agriculture and about 40 per cent of farmers are women, with about 20 per cent of rural households being *de facto* female headed due to widowhood, desertation or male out migration...inclusion of women or mainstreaming women in agriculture is likely to promote faster agricultural growth. In fact, the next phase of agricultural growth, which will have to focus on rainfed areas and dry land farming as well as on diversification of agriculture, will have to open up larger space for women as prime movers. Women will have to play an important role in crop cultivation, (common) natural resource management and in expediting agricultural diversification. Women's involvement as independent farmers and producers is not just for gender equity but also for faster and inclusive agricultural growth...It needs to be noted at the outset that gender is not a "sector" and therefore it cannot be discussed as if it is a separate economic activity. Gender is a cross cutting issue that needs to be mainstreamed in the strategy for agricultural development. Engenderment of agricultural strategy is necessary for faster and inclusive.

The Mahila Kisan Sashaktikaran Pariyojana (MKSP, 2011), which is a sub-component of the National Rural Livelihood Mission (NRLM) notes,

> Agriculture, the single largest production endeavour in India, contributing to 16 per cent of the GDP is increasingly becoming a female activity. Agriculture sector employs 80 per cent of all economically active women; they comprise 33 per cent of the agricultural labour force and 48 per cent of self employed farmers. About 18 per cent of the farm families in India, according to NSSO Reports are reported to be headed by women... Women in Agriculture are generally not able to access extension services and production assets like seed, water, credit, subsidy etc. As most of them are not recognized as farmers for want of ownership of land, they are not considered as beneficiaries of various government programmes/ services. The wage differentials between men and women being adverse to them, the situation is further aggravated. Some of the tasks performed by the women are not valued adequately and considered less important economically. Further, due to multiple roles that a woman has to perform within the family and the farm, her access to knowledge and information, is constrained and therefore her opportunities get limited.

This inequity mirrors a global reality. The FAO report (2011), states that women comprise, on average, 43 per cent of the agricultural labour force in developing countries. This ratio varies from region to region, but one feature remains common—this is the gender disparity in terms of access to assets, productive resources, inputs and services. 'If women had the same access to productive resources as men, they could increase yields on their farms by 20–30 per cent. This could raise total agricultural output in developing countries by 2.5–4.0 per cent, which could in turn reduce the number of hungry people in the world by 12–17 per cent.' IFAD (2011) puts it succinctly in a sentence, 'IFAD believes that rural poverty is deeply rooted in the imbalance between what women do and what they have.'

The Rural Baseline in India and Rural-Urban Linkages

Krishna and Bajpai (2011) explores rural livelihood in terms of rural-urban linkages. This study shows that economic impulses have a short span of 5 to 10 kms. This strongly reinforces the need for a local livelihood security approach.

Triangulating results from large household surveys conducted by the National Council of Applied Economic Research (NCAER) in 1993-94 and in 2004-05, and the Census 1991 and 2001 figures, Krishna and Bajpai (2011) concludes,

> The distribution of benefits from economic growth since the early 1990s has followed an identifiable spatial pattern. People in the largest cities have achieved the greatest gains, followed by people in small towns and villages close to towns. Further away, in villages located more than five kilometres from the nearest town—home to more than half of the entire population of India—inflation-adjusted per capita incomes fell between 1993 and 2005. The steepest declines were experienced by the lowest income groups. Rising inequality is a natural result of these spatially distributed trends. The debilitating effects of "distance from town" need to be countered by connecting outlying villages with more and better physical and social infrastructures.

This study categorises rural areas located adjacent to towns within a distance of five kms as the 'umbra' and affirms that this population segment (constituting 13.1 per cent of the rural Indian population according to the Census of 2001) has benefitted from national growth during the post-liberalisation period. 'Every income quintile in umbra villages increased its purchasing power, with the richest groups experiencing the largest, and the poorest groups experiencing the smallest, percentage increase' (Ibid.).

Villages outside the five km perimeter have been categorised as the 'penumbra'. Within the 'penumbra', villages located between 5 and 10 kms from the nearest town accounted for 19.5 per cent of the rural population in 2001 and villages beyond 10 kms from the nearest town accounted for 67.5 per cent of the entire rural population.

> In penumbra villages, as well, the richest groups grew richer, albeit not to the same extent as the richest groups in umbra villages. However, every other quintile has become poorer than before. The poorest groups in penumbra villages have seen their purchasing power fall by more than one-sixth over the same 12-year period (Ibid.).

> Poverty has been reduced within umbra villages, but it has simultaneously increased within penumbra villages...in villages located between five and 10 kilometers from the nearest town, the percentage in poverty went up by 5.6 per cent over this 12-year period, while still further away, more than 10 kilometers from towns, the increase in poverty was higher, 6.2 per cent. The sorriest part is that the vast majority of rural Indians live within such penumbra villages, more than five kilometers from the nearest town... More than 95 per cent of the rural populations of Andhra Pradesh, Orissa, and Jharkhand, and more than 90 per cent of the rural populations of Bihar, West Bengal and Chhattisgarh, live in villages located more than five kilometers from the nearest town. These people have seen their purchasing power drop, even as the country as a whole has grown rapidly. That they might experience discontent and disenchantment becomes easier to fathom (Ibid.).

> Instead of being mitigated, these disadvantages of distance have been compounded by public policies. Critical infrastructure has been located preferentially in close-to-urban villages...Consequently, people in further away villages have faced a harder time in making connections with market-based opportunities (Ibid.).

The study draws attention to three contemporary trends to explain why rural assets and incomes are both patterned radically differently in the villages in the umbra and in the penumbra, the nature of the handicaps suffered by the penumbra villagers and why distance to town matters so much?

First, is that the villages closer to towns have been able to leverage better, supplementary incomes from the non-agricultural sources during this period of decline in the amounts received per capita from agriculture (both in relative and absolute value) as a result of slow agricultural growth and a preponderance of tiny and uneconomic family plots due to sub-division of landholdings with each passing generation.

> While people of the lowest quintile in umbra villages—because of their proximity to towns and assisted by superior infrastructure—have been able to avail themselves of non-agricultural labour opportunities (in addition to undertaking agricultural labour in their villages), the lowest income

> quintile in villages beyond 10 kilometers from the nearest town have had to rely more centrally on agricultural labour, thus limiting their earning potential...relatively richer villagers have increased their holds on the most lucrative urban opportunities, arising from salaried and professional occupations (Ibid.).

Second, is the differential provision of critical infrastructure. Between 1991 and 2001,

> The percentage of villages connected by paved roads went up from 42 per cent to 64 per cent, and the proportion served with electric power went up from 68 per cent to 76 per cent. But such growth was disproportionately located in umbra (or inner-circle) villages...While 67 per cent of villages within five kilometers of towns were connected by paved roads in 2001, the corresponding proportions in villages 21-30 kilometers and more than 50 kilometers from towns were much smaller, 49 per cent and 34 per cent, respectively. Similarly, while more than 84 per cent of umbra villages were served by power supply, this proportion fell to 59 per cent in villages located furthest from towns. Poorer roads and greater distance working together considerably raise the transaction costs that have to be incurred by people from penumbra villages (Ibid.).

Third, the study notes,

> The rising premium to higher education and superior skills, the preferential location of high schools and colleges in towns and villages closer to towns (and the greater ability of richer villagers to acquire higher education (no matter at what distance), helps explain further the growing gap between richer and poorer villagers and among villages located closer to and further from towns...the proportion of households in which one or more adults have secondary or higher falls from 48 per cent in the nearest villages to 35 per cent in villages at the greatest radial distance from towns. In each band of village, however, this proportion is, not surprisingly, greatest among the highest income groups. Differences in educational ability are related to the ease of access that people in nearer and further villages have to high schools and colleges... As recently as 2008, DLHS-3 data show, people from penumbra villages needed to travel, on average, 12 kilometers in order to attend higher secondary schools, more than twice the distance that umbra villagers needed to travel for the same purposes. The difference in distance to college between umbra and penumbra villages is also large and significant: 12 kilometers *versus* 22 kilometers (Ibid.).

While according to this study, the proportion of rural population in umbra villages could have increased from 13 per cent in 2001 to 31 per cent in 2008 and the proportion living in the furthest-out villages (more than 10 kms from the nearest town) may have fallen even more drastically (by as much as 25 percentage points), the authors are not hopeful that the autonomous growth of markets, and with it, the spread of towns, will bring progressively more villagers within the beneficial inner circle. The study notes,

> Unfortunately, the data do not support any such optimistic prognosis. While towns have, in fact, advanced, the bad news is that towns have gone where market forces have taken them, following the money, while largely avoiding marginal areas with greater concentrations of poorer people. In 2008, for example, villages beyond five kilometers of towns accounted for 69 per cent of the entire rural population, but even greater proportions of poorer people—more than 75 per cent of scheduled castes, 83 per cent of scheduled tribes and 73 per cent of below-poverty-line households—lived within such villages. It seems too much to hope that the expansion of towns in the future will automatically correct these trends (Ibid.).

The study (Krishna and Bajpai, 2010) concludes,

> the question of exclusion of many has to be addressed. Unless investments in high-quality physical and social infrastructure are simultaneously made that connect outlying areas with the mainstream of growth, inequality will continue growing, and inclusive growth will remain a distant dream... Currently, too little is being done in this regard in India, and as a result, "in terms of inequality of opportunity and intergenerational mobility", India may well be on the way to becoming "one of the worst [countries] in the world" (Bardhan, 2010: 132).

Rural Livelihood and Rural Governance

The Constitution (73rd Amendment) Act, 1992 and the provisions of the Panchayats (Extension to the Scheduled Areas) Act, 1996 set the path for political decentralisation and enhanced participation of the community in planning and implementation of local development initiatives.

While there are vast expectations from this tier of grassroot democracy, its progress has been mixed and states/Union Territories (UT administrations are at varying stages in the implementation of the said Acts. This uneven progress has generated intense public debate on the role of the *panchayati raj*. Many see it as the panacea for ensuring dignity and decent livelihoods for the masses in this large and diverse country. But there is a school of thought that is less enthusiastic about the role and prospects of *panchayati raj* because of the inherent danger of elite capture at the local level, and the bleak prospects for sharing of power by the bureaucracy and the state-level political leadership.

This debate continues to be inconclusive particularly on account of paucity in authentic data on the functioning of the panchayati raj institutions (PRIs). The 2008 Perception Survey by the National Council of Applied Economic Research (NCAER) sponsored by UNDP covering 16 poorest districts in the seven least developed (northern) states in India sought to bridge this information gap (NCAER, 2008).

Table 2.1

District-wise Distribution of Household Requiring Services from Various Institutions

District	*Panchayat*	*PDS*	*Anganwadi*	*School*	*Sub-Centre/ Hospital*	*Doctor*	*Court*	*Police*	*Total*
Barmer (Rajasthan)	99.5	100.0	61.0	63.0	99.0	98.0	10.0	18.0	100
Dungarpur (Rajasthan)	98.0	98.5	44.5	47.5	87.0	68.0	3.0	8.5	100
Sitapur (UP)	94.0	100.0	29.0	55.0	74.5	74.5	7.0	7.0	100
Lalitpur (UP)	87.0	100.0	16.5	53.5	80.0	80.0	7.0	11.0	100
Azamgarh (UP)	67.0	100.0	19.0	76.0	35.5	71.5	4.0	2.0	100
Mandla (MP)	98.0	100.0	48.0	67.0	36.5	88.0	3.5	2.5	100
Tikamgarh (MP)	48.5	97.0	37.0	73.5	37.5	58.0	4.5	1.0	100
Gaya (Bihar)	64.0	99.0	46.5	68.5	90.5	83.5	8.5	4.5	100
Muzz.Pur (Bihar)	49.0	99.5	55.0	52.0	96.5	85.5	5.5	16.0	100
Purnia (Bihar)	29.5	84.0	48.5	66.0	82.5	77.5	3.5	3.5	100
Palamu (Jharkhand)	75.0	99.0	22.5	54.5	11.5	28.0	2.0	1.5	100
Dumka (Jharkhand)	65.0	100.0	29.0	50.5	9.0	25.5	0.0	0.0	100
Kanker (Chhattisgarh)	90.5	99.5	23.5	47.0	21.0	23.5	1.0	0.0	100
Bilaspur (Chhattisgarh)	80.0	99.5	23.5	62.5	33.0	20.0	1.0	0.5	100
Ganjam (Orissa)	89.0	98.5	57.5	61.0	55.5	97.0	20.5	20.5	100
Keonjhar (Orissa)	98.0	86.5	83.0	82.0	85.0	96.5	23.0	23.5	100
Total	77.0	97.6	40.3	61.2	58.4	67.2	6.5	7.5	100

Source: NCAER (2008).

The NCAER survey report shows that despite numerous teething problems, PRIs have come to occupy an important role in the lives of the poorest sections in India. Overall, 77 per cent of the respondents indicated that they needed services from *panchayats*. It is noteworthy, that the importance attached to *panchayats* was rated next only to the public distribution system (PDS), and higher as compared to institutions such as schools and hospitals. However, unlike the consistency seen in the case of PDS, the importance attached to *panchayats* varies considerably across districts—from 99.5 per cent in Barmer in Rajasthan to 29.5 per cent in Purnia, Bihar.

The data below classified caste-wise, shows some variability across castes. The ST (Scheduled Tribes) community attaches the highest importance to services from *panchayats* while the score in this regard by the SC (Scheduled Castes) community is comparatively lower.

Table 2.2

Caste-wise Distribution of Households Requiring Services of Various Institutions

Caste	*Panchayat*	*PDS*	*Anganwadi*	*School*	*Sub-Centre/ Hospital*	*Doctors*	*Court*	*Police*	*Total*
SC	67.6	96.3	36.0	59.5	61.0	65.2	4.1	5.4	100.0
ST	84.7	97.8	44.2	60.1	52.6	61.1	5.4	6.0	100.0
OBC	79.3	98.7	39.0	64.1	59.0	76.7	9.8	11.5	100.0
Others	76.2	98.7	32.3	47.7	52.6	55.4	9.2	8.9	100.0
Total	77.0	97.6	40.3	61.2	58.4	67.2	6.5	7.5	100.0

Source: NCAER (2008).

The *panchayats* also secured a good report card in terms of approachability.

Table 2.3

Approachability of Panchayats: Caste–wise Distribution of Respondents

Caste	*Very Easily Approach-able*	*Easily Approach-able*	*Approach-able*	*Difficult to Approach*	*Very Difficult to Approach*	*Total*
SC	32.1	46.8	12.4	6.3	2.3	100.0
ST	26.5	45.9	18.6	8.1	0.9	100.0
OBC	29.8	43.7	17.8	5.9	2.8	100.0
Others	30.2	45.8	16.2	7.3	0.6	100.0
Total	29.2	45.7	16.4	7.0	1.8	100.0

Source: NCAER (2008).

Table 2.4 shows the perception of the people on the role of various institutions in solving the common problems and issues confronting them.

Table 2.4

Community Perception on the Role of Institutions

Issues	*Institutions*						
	Panchayat	*Police*	*Community*	*Govt. Officials*	*Village Elders*	*NA/ No Res.*	*Total*
Law/order problems	25.9	55.1	1.9	3.8	5.2	7.9	100.0
Personal calamity	40.6	5.4	17.8	0.8	31.9	3.5	100.0
Wage dispute	70.4	1.7	4.1	5.4	12.0	6.3	100.0
Govt. programmes	46.0	2.8	6.0	27.0	3.7	14.5	100.0
Problems with other communities	36.2	6.5	25.6	4.9	19.3	7.4	100.0

Source: NCAER (2008).

In the context of the government programmes, the score for *panchayats* was 46 per cent as compared to a score of 27 per cent for government officials. This finding shows that in the eyes of the community, *panchayats* have a crucial role to play in making the government programmes deliver. Overall, this NCAER Perception Survey establishes that *panchayats* have emerged as a key institution in the rural landscape.

Yet paradoxically, this tier of democracy has not been able to leverage fully on its strength from below. The PPPP report (Singh, 2010) which explored this paradox argued that PRIs have not been able to occupy the governance space warranted by their growing base in rural masses because of the limited role that they see for themselves in agriculture which is the mainstay of the rural economy. The case study on Haryali Kissan Bazar in Ladawa, Karnal presented the results of a focus group discussion with a dozen *sarpanchs* to support this conclusion. The focus group discussion showed that even in the context of an agriculturally advanced region, 'the sarpanchs indicated that their main role was to resolve local disputes and to implement small works sanctioned by the Government. They explicitly declined any significant role for themselves in the development of agriculture' (Singh, 2010).

The PPPP report concluded,

> PRIs will not be able to gain their true place in the rural economy unless they accept a direct leadership role in agriculture which is the mainstay of the rural economy. But as the case studies in this report show, currently this appears to be the weakest link in many of the States. Weak convergence of programmes such as MGNREGS which PRIs are implementing may also flow from this lop-sided vision. The PPPP-based rural service enterprise model outlined above appears to be a timely solution to this imbalance. A mainframe monitoring role and responsibility for PRIs under the proposed paradigm will be an opportunity to equip them with suitable resource support. Presently, this is a crippling constraint.

The women and NRM survey in Dungarpur carried out under this follow-up study points to the need for a direct and active role for PRIs in rolling out a local livelihood security-based approach to rural prosperity.

3 The Women and NRM Survey in Dungarpur

Sample Characteristics and Survey Methodology

Sample Villages

The women and NRM survey carried out in May-June 2011 covered 190 women farmers across eight villages in the Dungarpur district of Rajasthan.

In terms of the Human Development Index (HDI), Dungarpur figures in the bottom pile of districts not only in Rajasthan, but across the country. With an HDI score of 0.409 in 2007, its HDI rank was 32 out a total of 33 districts in Rajasthan. According to the data provided by the Rajasthan Directorate of Economics & Statistics, the HDI score of Dungarpur infact shows a declining trend from 0.456 in 1999 to 0.409 in 2007, while during this period, the HDI of Rajasthan reportedly improved from 0.581 to 0.677.[1]

About two-third of the Dungarpur's population belongs to the ST category. The choice of Dungarpur for the women and NRM survey is based on the considerable baseline work done by CII under its Dungarpur PPCP initiative which aims at evolving models and demonstrating workable modalities for stimulating development of backward districts through win-win partnership between the business sector, vulnerable communities and public agencies.

1. Rajasthan Directorate of Economics & Statistics, *http://statistics.rajasthan.gov.in/socio_economic.htm*

Box 3.1

Dungarpur District: An Overview

The Dungarpur district located in the southernmost part of Rajasthan is spread over 3,856 sq kms. The tribal population constitutes around 65 per cent of the total. More than two-thirds of the district is highly undulating resulting in high surface run-off. The climate is generally dry with average temperatures during winter and summer varying from 5 to 45° C. Out of the total geographical area, only one-third is under cultivation and another one-sixth is forest land.

The average annual rainfall is 729 mm. Also, there are huge annual fluctuations. Recharge to the ground and biomass are poor. The existing groundwater potential has also not been tapped fully due to the poor economic status of the tribal dominated population. Out of the past 67 years, drought was experienced 15 times—this works out to a frequency of once in four years. Acute drought or near acute drought situation (less than 55% of rainfall) occurred six times (once in 11 years). In other words, drought occurs once in a four-year cycle followed by acute drought conditions in the next cycle.

The primary livelihood sources in Dungarpur district comprise agriculture, animal husbandry and forest produce. But the overall land productivity is rated to be low as compared to the neighbouring areas bordering Gujarat. This natural resource baseline has resulted in high degree of migration to other districts and states. Dungarpur is known for its migrant unskilled labour in the states of Gujarat, Bihar, Maharashtra and Madhya Pradesh.

Migration, unemployment, poor literacy (48.6%, male: 66.0% and female: 31.8%) and education (1,631 schools for 313,738 students) and lack of hospitals (123 nos.) have contributed to high infant mortality (IMR) and maternal mortality rate (MMR).

Table 3.1 presents the socioeconomic profile of the sample villages. It is clear that the socioeconomic baseline of these villages typifies a scenario of multidimensional poverty and human development deprivation.

Village Charwada is a *panchayat* headquarter having five revenue villages. Village Balwaniya is also a part of this *panchayat*. Geographically, the Charwada *panchayat* is a part of the Simalwada *tehsil* and Bichhiwada Block. It is about 25-30 kms from the district headquarter and about 8 km from the *tehsil* headquarter. It is a highly interior part of the district having poor road connectivity. Unlike other villages, agriculture and migration are the major sources of livelihood. The continued effort made by the

Confederation of Indian Industry (CII), the International Crops Research Institute for the Semi-Arid Tropics (ICRISAT) and People's Education and Development Organisation (PEDO) has improved agriculture to a certain extent. Efforts have also been made to improve irrigation availability through the water user group modality. Crops like maize cultivated during the rainy season and wheat during the winter season are the major food crops. Those who have irrigation facility are also cultivating winter crops. Some of the ancient water-lifting devices used for irrigation such as the tipping bucket and persian wheel are still being used by a few poor tribal families. These two villages are tribal dominated, and low male and female literacy level is an area of concern.

Table 3.1

Socioeconomic Profile of Selected Sample Villages

Gram Panchayat (Block)	*Charwada*	*Balwaniya*	*Renta*	*Juda*	*Mewada*	*Rampur*
Total population	1646	1471	1357	879	469	825
Total household	281	243	205	157	105	137
Total male	805	744	662	436	241	414
Total female	841	727	695	443	248	411
Total SC	6	0	0	0	136	0
Total ST	1344	1175	1326	865	143	663
Total literacy (%)	35	39	30	36	51	37
Male literacy (%)	48	57	42	55	58	49
Female literacy (%)	22	21	18	18	39	25
Land use (ha)						
Total area	431	331	458	252	60	124
Forest	16	21	0	0	0	0
Cultivable land	232	159	166	112	44.4	102
Cultivable waste	118	122	37	96	0	5
Not available for cultivation	65	69	253	43	5.58	17
Non-irrigated area	216	115	126	66	33	70

Juda and Renta are revenue villages, under the Renta *panchayat*. Both these villages were covered under the survey. The Renta *panchayat* is a part of the Dungarpur block and is about 25-30 km from the district head quarter. The villages have very poor road connectivity. The population of both the villages is predominantly tribal. Farming, which is mainly rainfed in nature and migration are the two major sources of livelihood. Both villages are situated on the ridge line of a watershed. Therefore, a major portion of the rainwater flows as a runoff leaving a water scarce situation in winter and summer. A small irrigation tank in the area has provided some respite from water scarcity for winter irrigation. Irrigated agriculture is mainly observed in and on the banks of major drains and canals, and in the command area of minor irrigation tanks.

Mewada shares borders with Gujarat. The influence of Gujarati culture on the local community is clear. Cotton seed farming has been adopted by most of the farmers in this area. This is a skill-intensive activity and requires specific skills for pollination. But the farmers in this bordering village have been successfully performing this task and earning a good amount. Migrant child labour was a big problem in this area, but now due to improvement in agricultural practices and earnings, child migration has been controlled to a great extent.

Rampur is a revenue village and a *panchayat* headquarter situated about 45 km from the district headquarters. It also shares a border with Gujarat. The influence of Gujarati culture on the local community is clearly seen particularly in terms of agricultural practices. The farming community in this border village is more innovative and competitively forward in adopting new technologies suitable for the area. The village is well connected by road. The livelihood system is mainly agriculture dependent and partly supported by migrant income earned from labour work in Gujarat.

The Sample Population

Table 3.2 outlines the socioeconomic characteristics of the sample population. About 93 per cent of the respondents belonged to the ST (scheduled tribes) category and about 87 per cent fell under the BPL (below poverty line) category. Thus, it is clear that this sample represents a segment that is at the core of India's inclusive growth concerns.

The land ownership pattern in the sample population presented in Table 3.3 shows that about 52 per cent of the respondents have land holding below three *bighas* or half hectare. A little less than half of the respondents own three *bighas* or more. Thus, three *bighas* or half an acre appears to be a good average landholding size in the target population.

Table 3.2

Profile of Respondents

Village	Gram Panchayat (Block)	Distribution of Respondents						
		Total	ST	SC	Others	APL	BPL	Antodaya
Charwada	Charwada (Bicchiwada)	28	28				27	1
Balwaniya	Mewara (Bicchiwada)	23	23			1	22	
Reta	Reta (Bicchiwada)	25	25			2	20	3
Juda	Reta (Bicchiwada)	26	26				22	4
Mewada	Mewara (Bicchiwada)	25	25			3	20	2
Rampur	Rampur (Bicchiwada)	25	25				23	2
Karkoli	Amritiya (Aspur)	19	5		14	10	9	
Oda	Lodawal (Aspur)	16	16			7	9	
Pachalasa Bada	Pachalasa Bada (Aspur)	3	3			1	2	
Total		190	176		14	24	154	12

Table 3.3

Pattern of Land Ownership in the Sample Population

Village	Gram Panchayat (Block)	Pattern of Land Ownership (in Bighas)							
		0-0.25	0.25-0.5	0.5-0.9	0.9-1.1	1.1-1.5	1.5-2.0	2.0-3.0	3-0 +
Charwada	Charwada (Bicchiwada)	-	-	-	2	3	3	3	17
Balwaniya	Mewara (Bicchiwada)	-	-	-	1	-	3	4	15
Reta	Reta (Bicchiwada)	-	2	1	1	5	1	2	13
Juda	Reta (Bicchiwada)	-	-	2	4	3	2	2	13
Mewara	Mewara (Bicchiwada)	-	1	-	6	6	5	2	5
Rampur	Rampur (Bicchiwada)	-	-	-	10	3	1	8	2
Karkoli	Amritiya (Aspur)	-	2	-	2	1	1	3	10
Oda	Lodawal (Aspur)	-	-	-	-	2	-	1	13
Pachalasa Bada	Pachalasa Bada (Aspur)	-	-	-	-	-	-	1	2
Total		-	5	3	26	23	16	26	90

Survey Design and Methodology

The survey was designed based on three focus group discussions with women farmers. These discussions were facilitated by PEDO.

The selection of the target areas was based on the following considerations:

- Maximum coverage of remote areas where the basic amenities are largely not available and the exposure to the government machinery is minimal.
- Due representation to the rainfed and irrigated areas.
- Areas in which PEDO and CII are active so that suitable response is forthcoming.

The size of the survey was kept at 190 respondents with about 20 to 25 women farmer per village. While selecting the respondents, the following considerations were considered important:

- Representation to the ST and SC (scheduled castes) community in line with the demographic profile of the district.
- Representation on the basis of the socioeconomic status, e.g. APL (above poverty line), BPL, etc.
- Suitable coverage under the under the SHG movement led by PEDO and the PPPP programme of CII.

The survey was administered by the PEDO staff which is proficient in the local language and has extensive experience in dealing with women farmers and their livelihood and empowerment-related issues. CII staff was given the responsibility of monitoring the survey, of providing the required technical support and for compilation of the data.

4 Results of the Women and NRM Survey in Dungarpur

Women Farmers are not Residual or Workers by Default

This survey provides clear evidence against the notion that women farmers are 'residual workers' or that they work on farms by default because of the absence of other opportunities. It is important to highlight this finding at the very outset as the above notion is responsible for perpetuating a subsidiary status to women farmers despite the fact that they constitute a quarter to a half of the workforce in agriculture and allied activities.

About two-thirds of the women farmers surveyed indicated that their efforts into farming will go up if the spouse/other members of the household earned enough from other sources to take care of the family needs. Such an eventuality will provide them with additional resources to improve farming. Another 23 per cent indicated that there will be no change in their efforts. The proportion of respondents who indicated that their efforts in farming will come down as a result of availability of alternative avenues of income was less than 10 per cent.

Table 4.1

Women Farmers: Likely Impact of an Increase in Income from Other Sources on their Farming Efforts

Choices	*Response (No.)*
No change	54
It will come down as HH needs can be purchased	23
It will go up as I will have resources to improve farming	163
Other responses	
Total	240

Note: Some respondents opted for response in more than one category.

Complimentary evidence emerges from the response to the question, 'will you consider shifting to an urban area if your spouse/other members of the household found well paid employment there?' Nearly three-fourth of the respondents indicated that they are not likely to move to urban areas.

Table 4.2

Will Women Farmers Shift to an Urban Area if their Spouse/Other Members of the Household Found Well Paid Employment There?

Choices	*Response (No.)*
Yes	45
No	139
Can't say	
Total	189

With regard to the choice of vocation for their educated daughters, the most popular option was that of a teacher in a local school, followed by a local government official and professionals (doctor, engineer). This perhaps reflects a preference for stable salary incomes for their wards and does not dilute or conflict with the choices that the women farmers affirm in so far as their own occupation and lifestyle are concerned.

Table 4.3

Choice of Vocation for Educated Daughters

Choices	*Response Pattern*
A well informed farmer	18
A teacher in a local school	101
A local government official	37
A *panchayat* member	1
A political leader	1
A professional (doctor, engineer)	21
Others (specify)	1
Can't say	10
Total	190

The complete lack of interest in *panchayats* and politics as possible options for their ward is a matter of concern for the democratic path that India has chosen. However, an alternative explanation may be possible for this response pattern. Perhaps the respondents do not see *panchayats* and politics as 'vocations'. Thus, having only one choice for the response, they have exercised it for a more regular income earning opportunity. Nonetheless, this finding signals the need for deeper exploration.

Empowerment

Work Distribution

The distribution of workload between women and men in the household shows some areas of specific responsibilities but large areas of shared work. Land preparation with bullocks and operation of diesel engines are primarily in the domain of male members. Sowing, milking, selling of milk and taking care of animals fall primarily in the domain of female workers. There is sharing of workload in other agricultural operations with the respective shares varying somewhat across different activities. By and large, the element of hired labour is minuscule in this scenario of subsistence farming.

Table 4.4

Details of Work Distribution between Women Farmers and Other Members

Agriculture Work	*Male*	*Female*	*Equal Partici-pation*	*Hired Labour*	*Female & Hired Labour*	*Equal Partici-pation & Hired Labour*
Land preparation						
• With the help of bullocks	172	7	4	6		
• Land clearing by collecting stubbles, stones etc.	3	107	78	1		
Sowing	3	151	34			
Irrigation						
• Operating diesel engine	139	4	13	8		
• Watering the field	23	57	106	1		
Weeding	4	62	112	9	1	
Thinning	17	25	135	11		
Fertilisation	49	28	110		1	
Post-emergence application	44	2	5			
Harvesting	4	41	132	8	1	2
Threshing						
• Using machines	61	5	101	11	1	1
• Manual threshing	82	3	64	9		
Care of standing crop	87	10	60	8		
Grazing of animals	8	67	110	4		
Milking	7	161	14			
Selling of milk	38	97	22			
Care of animal health when sick	3	130	50	3		
Any other						

Table 4.5 shows the contribution of women and men in so far as 'other incomes' are concerned.

Table 4.5

Details of Other Incomes

Type of Income	*Who has Earned the Income?*						
	You	*Your Spouse*	*Others in the HH*	*You & Your Spouse*	*You & Others in the HH*	*You, Your Spouse & Others in the HH*	*Your Spouse & Others in the HH*
Migration income	3	36	38	1		1	2
NREGS	82	18	18	50	4	7	
Other local labour	31	19	14	18	1	2	
Business income	14	7	1	2		1	
Others (income from service)	12	5	1	10			

It is clear that mostly the men migrate for work. But in terms of local labour earnings, under NREGS and outside, women contribute a larger share. Similarly, as business incomes arise mostly from the sale of small animals and poultry, women who tend to such animals see themselves as earning a larger share in this category.

Control over the Use of Income

Table 4.6 presents the response of the women farmers on their control over the use of income. The response pattern indicates that in the tribal culture of Dungarpur, women largely control the use of the income including from sources such as migration in which mostly men are involved.

Table 4.6

Control over the Use of Income Earned

Type of Income	*You*	*Your Spouse*	*Others in the HH*	*You & Your Spouse & Others in the HH*	*You & Others in the HH*	*You, Your Spouse*	*Your Spouse & Others in the HH*
Sale of produce	78	20	3			21	1
Sale of animal	76	19	4			24	
Migration income	59	19	6	1		6	
NREGS	101	12	3		2	13	1
Other local labour	63	18	4			1	
Business income (grosser shop)	30	4	1			2	
Others (service)	17	2				1	

Participation in Decision-Making

Similarly, the response pattern to the question on decision-making across various activities shows a picture of equal participation between females and males. But there are some variations across this baseline of equal participation. Men seem to have a relatively more dominant say in hiring of equipment, hiring of labour, and in buying of fertilisers. On the other hand, women have a larger say in selling of vegetables and poultry.

Table 4.7

Participation in Decision-Making

Activity	*Male*	*Female*	*Equal Participation*
The crop to plant	32	18	140
Hiring of equipment	73	14	100
Hiring of labour	64	27	95
Buying seed/fertiliser	84	18	88
Buying goat	29	18	136
Buying cow/buffalo	2	2	132
Buying poultry	2	8	112
Selling vegetables	11	49	56
Selling goat	5	9	121
Selling cow/buffalo	4	5	124
Selling poultry	3	11	112
Taking credit	12	7	111

Recognition of Contribution as a Farmer and its Impact

Against this baseline of a reasonable degree of intra-household equity, an extremely interesting picture emerges when actors outside the household are introduced in the matrix.

Table 4.8 presents the response to the question, 'Do you consider that the following duly recognise your efforts and contribution as a farmer? The results show that while the efforts and contribution of women farmers are receiving due recognition within the family and in the neighbourhood, a diametrically opposite picture emerges with respect to agencies responsible for public administration and local governance. The local NGOs are also seen to be similarly lagging in recognising the efforts and contribution of women as farmers.

Table 4.8

Recognition of Efforts and Contribution as a Farmer

Categories	*Yes, Adequately*	*Yes, But Not Fully*	*Do Not Recognise*
Your spouse	98	20	16
Other members of the household	125	10	1
Other women farmers in the neighbourhood	120	10	6
Community leaders	58	30	48
Panchayat members	8	47	77
Local NGOs	11	42	81
Government functionaries at local level (e.g. *gram sewak*)	15	26	90
Government functionaries at the higher level (e.g. collector)	4	18	111
Political leaders (e.g. the MLA)	2	9	111

The next two questions go on to explore the implications of the above perception of stakeholders on empowerment of women farmers and on their work. Table 4.9 presents the response with respect to the question, 'in case your answers to the above are largely in 'yes, adequately' or 'yes, but not fully', then what according to you has been the result?'

Table 4.9

Women Farmers: Results of Recognition of their Efforts and Contribution as a Farmer

Choices	*Yes*	*No*	*Tick Upto Three that You Consider Most Important*
My self-worth has improved	129	4	127
My decision-making power at the HH level has improved	130	3	122
My decision-making power at the community level has improved	112	21	75
I am able to get more support for my farming activities	128	4	54
The burden on me has been reduced	114	17	18

The response pattern to this question is largely consistent with response pattern to the previous question on role recognition. A high degree of recognition of the role of women as farmers at the household level is seen as contributing to high self-worth and decision-making power at this level. Women farmers are of the view that this role recognition has also improved their access to resources and reduced the burden on them. A similar picture emerges in so far as the community is concerned.

It is also important to note the priority that women farmers attach to different aspects of their life, as an individual and as a worker. It is clear that issues of self-worth, empowerment and equitable participation in decision-making are of highest importance for the women farmers. These findings are important for the design of public programmes. They suggest that supply-driven programmes which focus on providing inputs and facilities need to give way to more participatory design and implementation.

The survey also included a question on the other eventuality, i.e., lack of recognition of the efforts of women as farmers and its implications. The response summarised below shows some negative impact, but these are outnumbered by contra-responses. There is some difficulty in apportioning these responses across differing positions in respect of different stakeholders. In hindsight, this question as well as the question above should have been drafted such as to draw out the attribution effect in an unambiguous manner.

Table 4.10

Results of Lack of Recognition of Efforts and Contribution as a Farmer

Choices	*Yes*	*No*	*Tick Upto Three that You Consider Most Important*
My self-worth has decreased	48	57	67
My decision-making power at the HH level has decreased	27	78	45
My decision-making power at the community level has decreased	36	68	52
I am not able to get required support for my farming activities	32	72	23
The burden on me has increased	30	70	24

Land Title and Empowerment

The issue of gross inequity in land ownership for women has received considerable attention in the development literature. Accordingly, this survey included a specific question to benchmark the status in this regard and to explore the implications.

The results seem to indicate that the tribal society in Dungarpur is much more equitous in this respect with as many as 149 of 190 respondents reporting individual or joint title in the family land. But the focus group discussion with PRI leaders presented in Chapter 5 outlines a more mixed picture.

The results affirm the importance that women farmers attach to the issue of title to land. It engages the minds of nearly two-thirds of the women farmers, and three-fourths see it as a factor that will help in their role as farmers by improving access to credit and benefits from government programmes such as training.

Title to land is also seen as positively related to increased voice for women in community affairs and in the political space.

Table 4.11

Land Title and Empowerment of Women Farmers

Choices	*Yes*	*No*
Do you have individual or joint title to your family land?	149	41
Do you think sometimes about the issue of land title in your name?	121	69
If you do not have the land title, has it caused some feeling of insecurity?	125	65
Do you think that having individual or joint title to your family land will help you in your role as farmer?	141	43
If so, how? By getting credit from banks?	129	30
If so, how? By getting opportunities for benefit from government programmes such as training?	117	32
If so, how? By increasing your voice in community affairs?	95	52
If so, how? By increasing your chances of being elected as a *panchayat* member/MLA?	46	28

Priorities in Decision-Making

Decision Variables

This survey explored the priorities of women farmers and the underlying decision variables in so far as farming activities are concerned. Table 4.12 presents the response to the question, 'What are the considerations in your mind while planning your farming activities?'

Ensuring suitable availability of food for the household and of fodder emerges as the overwhelming priority in this resource poor and fragile eco-environment. But ensuring best possible returns is also high in the list of priorities.

An interesting picture emerges when the responses with respect to maximising returns, minimising risks and containing input cost are mutually compared. The response of women farmers in favour of maximising returns is about four times higher than their response for the latter two aspects. It shows that women farmers are guided by the value maximisation proposition while paying due regard to issues such as household food security. In other words, the profile of decision variables emerging from this study points to a modern and informed decision-making approach. This is a very important finding as often dismal outcomes in the context of the poor and the socially marginalised sections/communities are confused for a lack of rational decision-making and choice. As a result, developmental interventions are misdirected. In particular, the above presumption militates against participatory programme design and decision-making. Choices get thrust upon the poor by policy makers and programme managers who think that the community does not know what is in their best interest. Caught in such circumstances, the communities also align their attitude to public programmes as fortuous gifts rather than as stable development support. The resulting poor outcomes tend to perpetuate the above (mis)belief. Thus, this book advances the case for transforming development support by evolving mechanisms for mutually agreed compacts.

Table 4.12

Considerations by Women Farmers While Planning Farming Activities

Choices	*Yes*	*No*	*Tick Upto Three that You Consider Most Important*
Ensuring suitable food availability for the HH	189		188
Ensuring suitable fodder	187	2	153
Ensuring best possible returns	172		105
Generating some cash income	163	12	60
Minimising risk of loss and indebtedness	150	13	25
Keeping inputs costs to the minimum	164	19	26
Keeping the labour burden yourself to a manageable level	140	36	19

Another important observation is that the livelihood imperatives in this resource poor and fragile eco-environment seem to completely override the labour burden on women farmers. There is a need to explore this in depth.

The development literature points to possible differences in the decision variables that guide males and females in farming and conservation activities. The survey sought to explore this aspect through the questions, 'Do you think that your spouse's response to the above will be different?' and 'In your view, what will be your spouse's main considerations while planning the farming activities?'

Table 4.13

Do You Think that Your Spouse's Response to Planning Farming Activities will be Different from Yours?

Yes	*No*	*Can't Say*
163	17	11

It is clear that women farmers perceive a significant difference in the approach between male farmers and women farmers. This was also clear from the focus group discussions where women farmers spoke of the preference of men for cash incomes. However, the following response pattern on the perceived main considerations of male farmers does not show any difference *vis-à-vis* the priorities that the women farmers saw for themselves. Perhaps, in the survey, this question was not administered correctly.

Table 4.14

Perception of Women Farmers Regarding the Considerations Important to their Spouse in Planning Farming Activities

Choices	*Yes*	*No*	*Tick Upto Three that You Consider Most Important*
Ensuring suitable food availability for the HH	188		186
Ensuring suitable fodder	187	1	154
Ensuring best possible returns	170		96
Generating some cash income	161	12	44
Minimising risk of loss and indebtedness	154	20	9
Keeping inputs costs to the minimum	165	14	13
Keeping the labour burden yourself to a manageable level	140	33	12

Women Farmers and Credit

This survey identified a strong propensity in the community for creating mechanisms and facilities that they considered necessary for improving their farming operations. Given the context of poverty and subsistence farming, suitable facilities for credit acquire great importance. Thus, the survey explored the baseline as well as the measures which the community considered necessary for a breakthrough in this vital arena.

The response shows that by and large, the sample community has a very cautious approach to credit. This may also be a case of limited access to credit due to a paucity of economic means. It is also not clear whether or not the responses below consistently include all credit sources—formal and informal?

Table 4.15

Frequency of Loans by Women Farmers in the Last Three Years

Choices	*Please Tick the Response*
None	123
Once	30
Twice	26
Three times	6
More than three times	3

Table 4.16 shows that women farmers mostly depend on their neighbours and relatives, and on SHGs for small loans. However, for large loans, banks and SHGs emerge as the two main sources.

Table 4.16

Credit Source of Choice

Credit Source	*Three Choices (Small Loan Amounts)*	*Three Choices (Large Loan Amounts)*
Bank	89	188
SHG	113	157
Local moneylender against jewellery	66	99
Advance from Adtiya with commitment to sell your produce to him	27	15
From neighbour	137	28
From relatives	117	40
Any other	13	

It is clear that taking credit is largely a joint decision of the household. Similarly, the household considers itself jointly responsible for repayment of the loan.

Table 4.17

Who Takes the Decision Regarding Credit?

Choices	*Male*	*Female*	*Both*
Who takes decision on credit source?	14	1	175
Who plays proactive role in repaying bank loan?	12	18	160

The main priority areas for credit are the livelihood activities of farming and animal husbandry. Education, health and social liabilities are other important areas for credit. About a fifth of the households reported having taken credit for meeting their food requirement.

Table 4.18

Activities for which Women Farmers Took Credit

Activity	*Tick Upto Three that You Consider Most Important*
Agriculture	185
Animal husbandry	131
Food	35
Health-related expenditure	53
Education	87
Social liability	46
Repay past debt	22
Well deepening	2

The response indicates a high degree of success in building sustainable assets through credit. Fifty-four respondents indicated that combining credit with other support measures such as training and technical support could further enhance the utility of credit. Nineteen respondents wanted the credit to be subsided.

Table 4.19

Credit and Building Sustainable Income Assets

Choices	*Yes*	*No*
Are you able to use the loan amount to create sustainable income assets for family so that need for repeated borrowing is reduced?	157	29
If yes, what assets? Please specify	Purchase milch animals: 18	
	Farm mechanisation for leasing: 7	
	Land grading & development: 4	
	Improved agri productivity by using improved agri inputs & tech: 25	
	Create irrigation facility: 35	
	Purchase of irrigation equipment: 7	
	Goat farming: 4	
	Grocery shop: 4	
	Vegetable production: 2	
If no, why not? Please specify	No idea: 13	
	Less land: 1	
	Agriculture volatile to weather: 1	
	Less land: 2	
	Loan required for house: 1	
	Nobody at home to use loan amount for income generation: 1	
Do you think that credit needs to be combined with other support to enable its best use?	Yes 103	No 61
If so, with what? Please specify	Training and technical support: 37	
	Training on irrigation system repair: 1	
	Loan with subsidy: 19	

Knowledge and Capacity Building Needs

Knowledge Base

About 93 per cent of women farmers responded in affirmative to the question, 'Do you think that you have the knowledge to derive maximum output from farming?' Yet, as responses to some related questions show, this remarkable confidence level co-exists with a strong propensity for absorption of knowledge as well as initiative for self-help. This combination of attributes in a stakeholder group confronting multiple vulnerabilities sends a powerful message for inclusive growth strategies and for programmes such as BRGF (Backward Regions Grand Fund). It calls for strategies that poise this stakeholder group as the driver of change rather than as passive recipients of welfare measures.

Table 4.20

Self-Perception about Knowledge to Derive Maximum Output from Farming

Choices	*Response (No.)*
Yes	164
No	17
Can't say	9

Exploring deeper into the knowledge and capacity building needs, the survey sought response on a detailed menu of agricultural operations. Again the responses display a high degree of confidence—this is clear from the highly nuanced understanding of both their existing knowledge and the gaps in such knowledge.

Table 4.21

Self-Perception about Awareness with Regard to Various Agricultural Practices

Techniques	*Fully Aware*	*Aware, But Not Adequately*	*Not Aware*
Use of flood irrigation method	44	33	58
Application of chemical fertilisers	106	26	4
Use of sprinkler technique	30	28	78
Use of drip technique	26	29	81
Use of furrow irrigation method	23	37	75
Use of border irrigation method	109	23	3
Good quality drainage network	110	19	6
Application of gypsum	38	36	59
Application of sufficient quantity of FYM	85	41	41
Green manuring	60	19	48

Measures Outlined by Women Farmers for Supporting them in Improving Farm Output

The response pattern to the question, 'What measures are required to support you in improving farm output?' shows that women farmers attach highest priority to various aspects relating to knowledge and capacity building. This goes against the popular grain of understanding that has resulted in faulty design of public outlays on welfare measures and mistargeting of public subsidies.

The response pattern also shows a high propensity for local cooperation in terms of sharing of equipment, water resources, as well as labour. Infact, the responses to the questions in this subsection chart out a concrete framework of cooperation for meeting the needs of farmers in this remote tribal region. The model that emerges has much wider relevance for pro-poor development.

Table 4.22

Measures Outlined by Women Farmers for Supporting them in Improving Farm Output

Choices	*Yes*	*No*	*Tick Upto Three that You Consider Most Important*
More knowledge about new farming techniques	177	4	144
More knowledge about new irrigation techniques	169	15	85
More knowledge about new seeds and inputs	186	1	114
Timely advice on what to sow based on weather forecast, likely water availability etc.	167	10	31
Timely supply of inputs that you are already using	185	2	46
Better equipment for irrigation			
• Large	20	9	5
• Medium	114	9	31
• Small	41	8	12
Better credit supply to buy equipment	158	19	24
Better credit supply to buy inputs	148	29	16
Mutual sharing of equipment at the local community level	138	32	8
Mutual sharing of water resources at the local community level	141	47	2
Mutual sharing of labour resources at the local community level	145	24	2
Better labour sharing at the HH level	153	16	8
Better knowledge about market prospects	159	8	10

Table 4.23 presents the response on the training needs. Overall, the results show that only 38 per cent of the women farmers covered in the

survey had received training. However, nearly three-fourth of those who participated in training had found it useful, and there was an overwhelming demand for covering both men and women farmers in the training programmes.

An analyses of the source of training support, shows that 27 of the 73 women farmers who received training had been covered in the programmes organised under the CII PPCP initiative. In other words, even presuming that all the others were covered under programmes organised by the relevant government agencies or by other agencies with support from the government, it is clear that the coverage of public programmes does not add up to not more than a quarter of the stakeholder population. This dismal baseline seen in the context of the highest importance that women farmers attach to knowledge inputs is a matter of great concern.

Table 4.23

Training Needs

Choices	*Yes*	*No*		*No Response*
Have you ever attended training programme?	73	117		
If yes, then did you find it useful?	10	5		8
Who arranged it?	Under CII Dungarpur initiative: 27 *Gram sewak*: 13 Agri supervisor: 1 Department of animal husbandry: 3 *Panchayat*: 2 Do not remember: 27			
Who should get priority in training in agriculture?	*Male* 3	*Female* 23	*Both* 158	*No Response* 6

Keeping in view the existing dismal baseline, what mechanisms and measures are required to ensure comprehensive coverage? What should be the structure of the capacity building support? Should the current approach of one-time and fixed-duration training be replaced by a comprehensive rural-service enterprise package that includes capacity building and problem solving support on an ongoing basis as also services such as the supply of inputs, credit marketing support etc? The survey provided feedback on these issues of key policy significance.

Irrigation Practices and Mechanisation

The survey also attempted to establish the baseline in respect of issues such as irrigation practices and mechanisation, and to garner the suggestions of women farmers on harnessing these to their advantage.

Table 4.24 summarising the response on irrigation practices shows that although this stakeholder group belongs largely to the BPL category, nearly two-third of the households have succeeded in creating their own irrigation facility. This demonstrates their resourcefulness. The element of resourcefulness is also clear from the evidence on local cooperation for meeting the needs for water. About 88 per cent of the respondents indicated that if they did not have their own irrigation facility they got water from the neighbour. This base of social capital is of great importance, and harnessed in a systematic way, it could help create a comprehensive 'rural service enterprise framework' at the local level.

A feedback of far reaching policy significance emerges from the response to the question, 'Do you think that assured irrigation facility to every farmer rather giving them any direct monetary help will be more helpful to improving her/his livelihood status?' About three-fourth of the respondents showed preference for assured irrigation facility over direct monetory help.

This powerful message from a predominantly BPL group should serve as an eye opener for policy makers. It indicates that inclusive development strategies need to move away from a generalised and wasteful subsidy-driven approach to one that strengthens the capacity and the resource/asset base of the masses.

The survey included two questions on the need for mechanisation services. The first question explored the need for such services to reduce the burden or drudgery for women farmers. The results show that mechanisation in certain aspects such as land preparation is considered necessary. But as investments in machines are lumpy and beyond the reach of small farmers, how should such services be organised?

Table 4.24

Irrigation Practices

Issues	*Yes*		*No*	*Please Tick the Response*		
Do you have your own irrigation facility?	115		75			
If yes, then do you have irrigation diesel pump set?	90		100			
If yes, what is its nature?	Small-50					
	Large-40					
If you had a choice then what you would have preferred?	Small-108					
	Large-40					
If you do not have irrigation facility, then do you get water from neighbour?	135		18			
If yes, then who initiate dialogue with them?	*You*	*Your Spouse*	*Others in the HH*	*You & Your Spouse*	*Any-body from Family*	*You & Others in the HH*
	46	46	29	9	8	2
Do you think assured irrigation facility to every farmer rather giving them any direct monetary help will be more helpful to improving her/his livelihood status?	*Yes*	*No*		*No Response*		
	125	35		30		

Table 4.25

Mechanisation Needed to Reduce Burden and Drudgery for Women Farmers

Activities	*Necessary*	*Not Necessary*
Machine for seed sowing	132	58
Machine for weeding	59	131
Machine for paddy transplanting	84	106
Machine for harvesting and threshing together for wheat	102	87
Machine for harvesting maize, paddy	83	106
Rain gun for irrigation	91	97
Machine for land preparation	152	35

The survey provides an answer to the above question. Ninety-eight per cent of women farmers showed willingness to pay for requisite mechanisation services, if prices were reasonable and if suitable credit services were made available. Again, this response points towards the need for a comprehensive rural-service enterprise package.

Table 4.26

If Mechanisation Service is Made Available in the Village, Would You Like to Take Benefit of it by Paying Competitive Services Charges?

Possible Responses	*Tick Upto Two of the Boxes*
Yes, I will pay if prices are reasonable	186
Yes, I will pay if suitable credit is made available	174
No, I will not pay as we can do the work ourselves	4

Benefits from Laws, Policies and Government Programmes

Laws and Government Policies and Women's Role as a Farmer

Over eighty per cent of the respondents answered in affirmative to the question, 'Do you think laws and governement policies are supporting women's role as a farmer?' However, a review of the examples outlined by women farmers shows that by and large, their responses relate to inputs and services from various sources.

Table 4.27

Are Laws and Policies Supporting Women Farmers?

Choices	*Yes*	*No*
Laws	154	36
Examples	- Seed supply in village (17) - Training to women farmer to impart knowledge of agriculture (12) - Fodder kit distribution (1) - SHG (6) - Loan through SHG for dairy (2) - *Gram sewak* calls for meetings (17) - Increased productivity (9) - NREGS scheme (6) - Seed production with SHG (2)	- Do not know (15) - Never got any kind of help (1) - No time to get information from *gram sewak* (1) - No training for females (1) - Nobody asked to participate in training (2)

Benefits from Government Programmes

The response to the question, 'Have you benefitted from the government schemes?' is of considerable importance as limited outreach of development programmes to the marginalised communities, particularly in the backward regions has been a core concern of inclusive growth strategies.

The response shows a mixed picture. Although the baseline in respect of human development services in the sample villages continues to be highly sub-optimal, a large proportion of women farmers report of progress in these areas.

Women farmers in this remote tribal region also report of benefits from increased availability of agricultural inputs and from knowledge about agriculture. However, it may be noted that the supply of agricultural inputs is largely in the private domain. Also as many of the reports including by the Farmers Commission have stressed, dissemination of knowledge is largely linked to input supply. The focus group meeting with PRI leaders presented in Chapter 5 indeed brings out that the progress has been more modest than the picture presented in these responses.

The responses report of low level of progress in many of the areas on which the livelihood of the poor depends. This includes forest cover, availability of water, fodder and credit.

Table 4.28

Benefits Derived from Government Schemes

Choices	*Yes*	*No*	*Tick Upto Three that You Consider Most Important*
Water availability in village	71	112	55
Forest cover	32	138	21
Agricultural inputs	167	18	127
Equipment for agriculture	78	97	41
Agriculture knowledge	126	60	82
Credit for agriculture	56	112	10
Fodder availability	65	103	27
Electricity availability	80	85	23
Health	144	29	61
Education	146	28	49
Transport	96	77	10
Better respect for farmers	52	116	10
Empowerment of weaker sections	37	129	2

An observation of considerable importance is the perceived low progress in empowerment of weaker sections and farmers. This finding is consistent with the response from women farmers highlighting the deficit in recognition from agencies outside their household, neighbourhood and their proximate community.

MGNREGS

The survey shows that 98 per cent of the respondents had a MGNREGS job card and about 94 per cent of those having job cards had participated in MGNREGS works.

Table 4.29 sums up the response on the impact of MGNREGS on the lives of people in sample villages. It shows that MGNREGS has played an important role in terms of ensuring food security of households in this fragile eco-environment. MGNREGS has also improved the financial condition of households and helped check distress movement of labour from this area known for rampant migration on account of deficient livelihood opportunities during the lean season. At the same time, the respondents are of the view that MGNREGS has reduced the supply of labour needed for farming activities.

MGNREGS in Dungarpur receives high scores in terms of equal opportunity to women and men. The score in terms of creation of village-level assets (e.g., village ponds and watersheds) are also moderately high. It appears that the considerable groundwork done by both the district administration and the NGOs in the context of planning, implementation and social audit under MGNREGS works has paid dividend.

Yet, the response points to low levels of transparency in the use of MGNREGS funds. The survey indicates that according to women farmers, women's groups could make better and more transparent use of MGNREGS resources.

The survey indicates that MGNREGS has improved social cohesion in the villages covered. However, with regard to its possible impact on self-confidence, while 34 respondents answered in the affirmative, more than double this number responded with a 'no'. This feedback needs deeper analysis.

Table 4.29

Benefits from NREGS

Choices	*Yes*	*No*	*Tick Upto Three that You Consider Most Important*
Helped to check migration of family members	130	56	118
Improved food security of the family	164	19	112
Improved financial condition of the family	175	11	124
Improved village-level assets (e.g. village ponds, watershed)	119	55	26
Improved self-confidence of village folk	34	80	1
Improved social cohesion in the village	135	36	17
There is transparency in the use of NREGS funds	39	131	5
NREGS has reduced the supply of labour needed for farming activities	134	39	31
Men and women get equal opportunity in NREGS	157	16	41
Women's group could make better plans for utilisation of NREGS resources	149	20	12
Women's group could implement NREGS in a more transparent manner	145	26	24

Evidence on Social Capital and its Far Reaching Implications

An important objective of the survey was to fathom the nature and strength of the social capital present and to explore the potential for public-private-*panchayat*-community partnership to uplift the livelihood baseline in this remote tribal region characterised by a fragile eco-system.

About 43 per cent of the respondents confirmed having participated in *gram sabha*. Such participation rate could be called moderately high by standards witnessed elsewhere in the backward regions.

Table 4.30

Participation in Gram Sabha

Choices	*Yes*	*No*
Have you ever participated in *gram sabha*?	80	106
If not, why?	No information about meeting reaches to us: 1 No time for such activity: 3	

Such moderately high participation levels in the *gram sabha* impart credibility to the response to the question, 'What are the main roles of *panchayats*?'

The response pattern indicates that the community expects *panchayats* to play an important role in local development activities such as creation of economic and social infrastructure and in the implementation of MGNREGS. But what comes as a surprise is the high expectation from the *panchayats* in the implementation of programmes to improve water availability and in making available other inputs including credit. In terms of importance, these items are ranked significantly higher than the traditional functions of *panchayats* such as resolution of local disputes and implementation MGNREGS.

Table 4.31

Responses on the Main Role of Panchayats

Choices	*Yes*	*No*	*Tick Upto Three that You Consider Most Important*
Implement programmes to improve water availability	168	21	138
Implement programmes to make available other inputs	164	13	131
Implement programmes to make available credit	140	35	74
Implement programmes to improve knowledge on farming	154	24	34
Make roads to improve connectivity	171	16	40
Establish more schools and hospitals locally	155	19	22
Implement NREGS more regularly	179	6	58
Create local employment opportunities so that the male members do not have to migrate out	143	29	18
Resolve local disputes	152	22	29
Empower and support women in their role as farmers	124	49	7

The survey indicates that there are a number of other forums in the village. The SHG (self-help group) modality dominates with about one-third of the women farmers being a member of one of the local SHGs.

Table 4.32

Committees Existing in the Village

Choices	*Which of the Following Committees Exist in Village?*	*In which Committees are You a Member? Please Tick*
Farmers groups	21	7
SHG	123	63
JFM	33	6
WUG	12	7
Health/education	14	1

Note: SHG: Self-help group; JFM: Joint forest management; WUG: Water user group.

Potential for Local Cooperation

The above background leads to an important set of questions on local cooperation around livelihood priorities.

The response to the question, 'Do you think that women farmers need to come together to create a support structure/SHG to get suitable services of agriculture experts, animal doctor, credit facilitator etc.?' marks an important departure from the traditional development discourse (Table 4.33). A positive response from over 90 per cent of the respondents signals the need for a fundamental rethink of the supply-driven approach to poverty alleviation. It shows that there exists a strong foundation of social capital and self-help initiative in this stakeholder group beset with multiple vulnerabilities. Developmental initiatives need to build on this strong foundation. This is the recipe for community ownership, local relevance, cost-effectiveness, impact, sustainability and inclusive growth.

Till now, self-help initiatives through the popular SHG mechanism have focused mostly on savings, credit and livelihood activities at a micro-scale and in a fragmented manner. The above response shows that it is possible to harness the self-help potential to forge larger institutional solutions such as a local extension machinery.

Table 4.34 summarises the response on the needs that a local group could help meet. It shows that knowledge about new farming techniques and timely supply of inputs being used emerged as the two main priorities for such local action. Better credit supply for procuring inputs and equipment and for creating irrigation facility, and support for knowledge about new seeds and inputs emerged as second order priorities.

Table 4.33

Do Women Farmers Need to Come Together to Create a Support Structure/SHG to Get Suitable Services of Agriculture Experts, Animal Doctor, Credit Facilitator etc.?

Choices	*Yes*	*No*	*Can't Say*
	172	11	7

Table 4.34

Three Most Important Needs that a Local Group Could Help Meet

Rank 1	*No*	*Rank 2*	*No*	*Rank 3*	*No*
More knowledge about new farming techniques	56	Timely supply of inputs that you are already using	17	Better credit supply to create irrigation facility	2
Loan to purchase equipments	3	Better equipment for irrigation	5	Better credit supply to buy equipment	15
Timely supply of inputs that you are already using	35	More knowledge about new farming techniques	24	Timely supply of inputs that you are already using	7
Better credit supply to buy inputs	2	More knowledge about new seeds and inputs	11	Better credit supply to buy inputs	14
More knowledge about new seeds and inputs	6	Better credit supply to buy equipment	17	More knowledge about new seeds and inputs	41
Irrigation facility	3	Better credit supply to create irrigation facility	2	Better knowledge about market prospects	5
Better equipment for irrigation	1	Better credit supply to buy inputs	30	Timely advice on what to sow based on whether forecast, likely water availability etc.	5
		More knowledge about new irrigation techniques	20	Better equipment for irrigation	8
				More knowledge about new farming techniques	8
				More knowledge about new irrigation techniques	1

It is clear that the women farmers feel the need for a convergent and continuing mechanism for making available a range of services. Thus for instance, the responses seem to caution against fragmented programmes for various agriculture-related needs. Similarly, they seem to caution against the current one-time and fixed duration training approach. These findings entail an important message for the design and structure of public programmes.

Around 85 per cent of the respondents wanted the support group to be set up at the village level. This reflects the importance that women farmers attach to local institutional solutions.

Table 4.35

Level at which the Group Needs to be Formed to Serve Best the Local Interest while Keeping Costs Manageable

Choices	*Response*
At the district level	11
At the block level	14
At the village level	164
Others (specify) *gram panchayat* level	3

The earnestness of the respondents regarding local institutional solutions on the above lines is also clear from the fact that 99 per cent of the respondents voted in affirmative to the question, 'If you are convinced that such a group will be in your long-term interest, will you contribute your share towards the costs, say ₹ 50 or 100 per year?' About 97 per cent of the respondents indicated that they will pay their contribution and in cash.

Table 4.36

Response on Willingness to Contribute for Creating and Maintaining the Local Group

Choices	*Response*
Yes	186
No	2
Can't say	

The survey delved deeper into the structure of the proposed institutional mechanism. The results show that about 95 per cent of the women farmers wanted a local agency to take the lead in setting up the local extension machinery. Around 66 per cent of the respondents wanted the local NGOs to take a lead. *Panchyats* and government functionaries at the local level were also cited by some respondents as possible initiators.

Table 4.37

Who should Set Up the Support Structure?

	Response (No.)
Would you prefer such a group to be set up by someone else?	
Yes	183
No	3
Can't say	7
If your answer is yes, then who should set up the support structure?	
Panchayat	54
Local NGOs	125
Government functionaries at local level e.g. *gram sewak*	39
Government functionaries at the higher level e.g. collector	3
Political leaders e.g. the MLA	

Note: Some responses ticked more than one item.

The response in favour of local initiative was overwhelming. It was duly backed by a resolve to contribute towards local mechanisms that generate long-term benefits to the community. These include: (a) an easily accessible agri-extension support structure and (b) mechanisation services. Similar responses showing a preference for assured irrigation facility over direct monetary help point to the need for a comprehensive re-look at the anti-poverty policies and programmes. In particular they calls for a shift from a shallow and fragmented subsidy regime to targetted support for community-led rural service enterprise models.

Role of Women's Leadership

The survey explored the role of leadership by women in carrying forward the development agenda emerging from the ranks of women farmers. It appears however, that the quality of data generated against some of the questions in this section is not satisfactory. This may be due to the lengthy nature of the questions as well as flaws in administering the questions. The analysis below should be considered with this caveat.

The response in favour of greater leadership role by women was unequivocal. About 90 per cent of the women farmers affirmed that greater leadership role by women will contribute to development.

Table 4.38

Will Greater Role for Leadership by Women Improve Development?

Choices	*Response (No.)*
Yes	167
No	13
Can't say	7

It is clear that leadership by women is seen in a highly positive light in all aspects of governance. In terms of attributes, more respect for women, greater concern with issues that impact women and better articulateness in expressing their demands received the highest scores. However, when rating the three features that they considered most important, the respondents showed an overriding preference for indicators that define approachability. This finding is in line with the feedback from women farmers that their role and contribution do not get due recognition outside their home and proximate community.

Table 4.39

Response on Positive Aspects of Womens' Leadership

Choices	*Yes*	*No*	*Tick Upto Three that You Consider Most Important*
Easy to approach	144	22	101
Have more respect for women	171	3	113
I would feel more comfortable in expressing/discussing things	158	10	118
Less corrupt	128	34	36
Will be more concerned with issues that impact women	163	5	56
Are more articulate in expressing their demands	166	2	45
Policy makers pay more attention to women's voices	154	13	17
Other	3		

Related to the above, the survey explored the qualities that women farmers would like to see in women leaders.

Table 4.40

What are the Qualities that You Would Like to See in Women Leaders?

Response	*No.*
Respect to women	4
Good leadership and gentle behaviour	13
Educated	59
Good speaker and thinker	15
Interest in social work and social thinking	17
Confident and courageous leadership	16
Feeling of equality	1
Knowledge of government schemes and new agri technologies	11
Hard worker	1
Trustworthy	5
Easy to approach	3
Young	1
Cooperative in nature	3
Transparent and unbiased leadership	19
Development-oriented attitude and focus on development	6
Knowledge of agriculture	8
Knowledge of animal husbandry	2
Good tolerance	1
Non-corrupt and able to provide good governance	2
Honesty	4
Total	191

The response to the vital question on the priorities that women farmers would like the women leader to address was unfortunately quite thin. But from the limited data that is available, it is clear that women farmers see an organisational role for women leaders in both the empowerment/awareness building space and in improving access to government programmes and resources (credit).

Table 4.41

Identify Priorities that You would Like Women Leader to Address?

Response	*No.*
SHG formation	1
Raise village problems at higher level	6
Create awareness and interest in society	12
Converge government schemes for village development	14
Health facility	3
Drinking water facility	3
Organise training and awareness campaign for women	9
Basic amenities in village	1
Create credit facilities in village for poor	8

Conclusion

A large volume of quality work is available on gender inequity in agriculture. This element is also visible in this survey even though it covers a predominantly tribal society which is considered to be relatively more gender equitable. But more important is the point of departure of this survey which is the innate dynamism and strength of the women farmers. These findings have far reaching implications for delineating a clear path in this era where the social goals and economic objectives have been brought into a point of confrontation. The concluding chapter dwells on this in some depth.

5 The Perspective of Women PRI Leaders

Introduction

A focus group meeting was organised with a dozen women PRI members from four *panchayats* covered under the survey. This group included two deputy *sarapanchs*. The purpose of the focus group meeting was to validate the findings of the village-level survey, and particularly to draw out the implications with regard to women's leadership as well as the role of PRI in taking forward the development agenda emerging from the village survey.

As outlined in the following, this exercise proved to be highly productive in that certain nuances that had remained dormant or blunted in the village survey emerged clearly from this relatively more empowered group. Particularly, a rich set of suggestions emerged on the way forward.

Women as Farmers

Recognition of Women as Farmers

The women PRI members agreed with the survey finding that their role as farmers is recognised by the spouse, other family members, neighbours and community leaders. They also agreed with the finding that their contribution as farmers did not get due recognition from the government machinery or from the MLAs. In support of this conclusion, they pointed out that in local or district-level trainings, the ground-level government staff preferred male farmers and invited only as many women farmers as is required by the government order—they 'never favour women farmers at large.' It emerged that even though village-level training camps were being organised from time to time, none of the women PRI members participating in the focus group had availed of training relating to agriculture. When asked about the reason for this gap, lack of information was cited as a major constraint. They indicated that sometimes even the *sarpanch* did not share with them information about such activities.

With regard to the fellow PRI members and local NGOs, the perception of women PRI members differed from those in the survey findings. They attributed this to their regular interaction with the fellow PRI members, community leaders and the local NGO staff.

Considerations while Planning Farming Activities

The women PRI members broadly agreed with the survey findings on the factors impinging upon the decisions of women farmers with regard to farming activities.

Land Title

In the village survey, nearly 80 per cent of the women farmers had reported that they enjoy joint land title. The women PRI members however, presented a much more humble picture. They confessed of a strong sense of insecurity because of lack of land title in a male dominated culture. Knowing that the spouse will not drag him into any legal battle, the male could easily seek seperation by paying a small amount. Female illiteracy played a role and bolstered the confidence of males. The women PRI members stressed that securing land title would help in establishing themselves as farmers. They could get bank loan easily and access government trainings. Also, land title will strengthen their role in social activities.

Access to Training

The women PRI members attach considerable importance to training in modern farming techniques. They want organisation of exclusive training sessions for women farmers. Also, they feel that the trainer must be a female who could listen to them carefully and work with illiterate women farmers with due patience. In the village survey, however, no particular preference had emerged for female trainers.

Farm Mechanisation

The PRI members stressed that it was the need of the time to adopt mechanised farming. Since farm machineries are costly and beyond the means of individual farmers, they suggested village-level equipment sharing arrangements. They expressed willingness to pay for such services.

The women PRI members were unanimous in stating that if all farmers got assured irrigation facility, they would not need any direct financial support for improving their livelihood.

Farming: A Way of Life

The women PRI members indicated that increased family earning will intensify efforts in agriculture instead of turning the focus away from it. Similarly, they echoed the survey findings that they would prefer to stay back in the village even if household members found lucrative jobs in nearby cities.

The women PRI members were highly enthusiastic about the prospects of education for their daughters. Eighty per cent of them wanted their daughter to become a teacher in a local government school whereas 10 per cent wanted their daughter to be a nurse. One of the PRI leaders wanted her daughter to pursue agriculture while serving in a local government school. The preference for secure livelihood in a local setting was apparent.

Perception on Government Policies and Programmes

The perception of women PRI leaders on the friendliness of the government policies and programmes towards women farmers differed from the response pattern in the village level survey. This difference in perception acquires particular importance as women PRI leaders are more exposed to government functioning.

Whereas as about 80 per cent of the respondents in the village survey had opined that government policies and programmes are friendly to women farmers, the women PRI leaders were of the view that government rules and policies are not friendly for promoting women as farmers. The PRI members explained that the respondents in the village survey might have considered government activities such as making available seed kits, fodder kits, MNREGS etc., as meant for women farmers only. Also, their positive response may have been based on formation of SHGs and their linkages to banks etc. But in reality, the SHGs formed by the government directly through the Integrated Child Development Services (ICDS), *Anganwadi* etc., are not functioning as well as those formed by the NGOs.

The women PRI members were of the view that knowledge of new farming techniques and inputs, timely advice on cropping choices based on the weather forecast, timely availability of inputs along with market-related knowledge are essential for the upliftment of those dependent on agriculture. They indicated that the governments should focus on these issues rather than on giving monetary benefits.

They also strongly affirmed that instead of providing support to individual beneficiaries, the government should create community-based resources in a manner that takes care of every beneficiary it is supposed to cater to.

Not a single women PRI leader was aware of the terminology of BRGF or of the fact that such a programme was being implemented in the district. This should be a valuable feedback about a programme cited by the Approach Paper to the Twelfth Plan as one the main planks for the development of backward districts.

When asked to comment on the nature of activities under the current BRGF plan which included mainly building works, they said that most of such works should be covered under other schemes implemented by various departments or under MGNREGS. BRGF should be used for the type of work which can't be covered under other schemes. Activities relating to the development of agriculture dominated the menu suggested by the women PRI members. These responses are discussed in Chapter 6.

Functioning of PRIs

The women PRI leaders expressed the need for a change in the present working style of PRIs. They indicated that the present methodology adopted by the field-based government functionaries and some PRIs to prepare village development plans was not proper and needed improvement. They stressed that the expected outcome/output of every action taken needed to be defined clearly and the role and responsibility of every stakeholder involved in planning, implementation and monitoring of the proposed village development plan should be clearly outlined.

They indicated that the majority of developmental works such as construction of water conservation structures, private land-levelling, distribution of agri-inputs, selection of beneficiaries for housing scheme and installation of handpump etc., are generally based on the demands of influential persons. Also, the work is implemented without considering its technical feasibility. Some *sarpanchs* adopt an appeasement policy to make their relatives happy. Transparency is not maintained in awarding work tenders and often these are either awarded to the relatives of the local government functionaries or to the relatives of the *sarpanch*. To avoid such weakness, transparency needs to be maintained in the *panchayat* functioning. One of the suggestions was to involve in such decisions, at least 20-30 per cent of individual community members, teachers, community leaders etc., so that 'every one will come to know about the decision taken by the *panchayat*.'

The women PRI members wanted the involvement of women leaders in planning and execution of works undertaken by PRIs and were confident that women could play an important role. They felt that women PRI members who are active should be given more responsibility in *panchayat* work. Further, they wanted the government employees working with them to explain every scheme and its functioning properly in easy and understandable language and also give due weightage to their suggestions.

The women PRI members wanted support for enhancing their working efficiency. They felt that *panchayats* should organise training and exposure for women PRI members so that their thought process became wider and more comprehensive.

Women Leadership

It was evident from the interaction that women PRI members were highly aware of the power and usefulness of unity. They said that it was necessary for women farmers to come together to avail of services such as agricultural extension, support for animal husbandry, credit etc.

They were of the view that an SHG like mechanism will be most suited for meeting their needs in agriculture. They stressed that they will not hesitate in paying a membership fee on the lines of the fees that they were paying for meeting the administrative expenses of existing SHGs.

The women PRI members were categorical that leadership by women was necessary for equitable and sustainable development. A few of the members explained that women generally adopt fair practices as compared to their male counterparts. This begets respect from women farmers. Hirki Behn, the deputy *sarpanch* of the Kakaradara *panchayat* said, 'I often tell my husband that it is my work and I am capable of doing it.' She said that she also encourages fellow women PRI members to attend trainings/ functions alone and not to bring their husband. At times, she had forcefully made the husbands of fellow PRI members to go back.

When asked about the three top priorities that women leaders needed to address, the women PRI members listed the following: year-round availability of clean drinking water, quality education in villages, work towards resolving issues relating to agriculture with major focus on availability of irrigation to all and supply of quality agri-inputs.

They unanimously cited another priority area. This was to discuss thoroughly during *panchayat* general meetings, every activity/scheme proposed to be implemented in the village and to incorporate genuine issues related to village development without any bias.

With regard to the measures required to promote women's leadership, many of the participants suggested that in all functions at the *panchayat* level, women leaders need to be given preference and invited to speak before any male member shared his views. Similarly, during village meetings/ planning process, women should be given the first chance to list activities/ views that they feel are important. Second, dedicated training programmes and exposure visits for women leader/farmers should be planned. Third, regular and thorough discussions should be organised at the *panchayat*, block and the district level involving women leaders in various government schemes including the content of the schemes, mode of implementation, role of various stakeholders, grievance redressal mechanism, selection of beneficiaries etc. Such discussions were required for strengthening the knowledge base of women leaders.

Creation of a Community-based Extension Support System

The women PRI members were of the view that a separate and effective institutional mechanism for agri-extension services was required. All women farmers could be included through small groups based on considerations such as the type of crop grown, irrigation source, geographical boundaries etc. About 20-30 women farmers could form a 'common interest group' (CIG). These CIGs would be the basic unit for the proposed extension system. This mechanism should follow the same route as the SHGs. A CIG could be headed by a nominated president and a vice-president as in SHGs.

The second step in the extension system hierarchy should be a village council comprising members nominated from the village-level CIGs, the *gram sewak*, the *panchayat* secretary and NGO representatives. The village council's responsibility should be to prepare the village-level action plan and secure its approval through the *panchayat* general meetings. The government should make it mandatory to incorporate in every village development plan or scheme, the suggestions of the village council forwarded through the proper channel.

After this ground work is done, the plan prepared could take its own route e.g. the agriculture assistant should forward the plan developed for agriculture to the Agriculture Department. Similarly, the *panchayat* secretary should forward the plan for rural development to the Block Development Officer (BDO). Likewise for areas relating to forests, electricity, health etc.

The third level of the hierarchy will be a cluster council. The cluster council would comprise mainly representatives of village councils, NGO representatives and cluster-level government officials etc. The major role of the cluster council will be to provide back-end support to concerned village councils in all activities including planning, execution and monitoring, as also to identify the training needs of the village councils. The cluster council should continuously follow up with all the relevant departments.

A number of cluster councils will form a block council in which block-level officers of departments mainly associated with developmental activities, NGO representatives, representatives of cluster councils, representatives of village group etc., will participate. The block council will be responsible for the smooth functioning of the clusters as well as village councils.

A key part of the extension machinery will be a district council which will be formed by the representatives of the councils at the village, cluster and block levels, district heads of concerned departments and the heads of local NGOs. It will be headed by 'the most responsible person of the district—Collector or Assistant Collector of the district.' The main responsibility of the district council will be to provide market linkages, technical support linkages, input linkages to the extension system, to take care of disputes if any, monitor the progress of work assigned to individual departments in the village development plans or schemes, the quality of agri-input supplies etc. The district council could also include representatives of industries, mainly those supplying seeds, fertilisers, pesticides, equipment manufacturers, agro-processing industries etc. Preference will be given to those who are registered or approved by the district agriculture department.

The women PRI members stressed that the government will have to make it mandatory for every department to incorporate the suggestions of the village council in every plan. The suggestions will be routed through the proper legal channel so as to avoid any communication gap and to promote transparency.

According to the women PRI members, the funding for the maintenance of the above mechanism could come out of the membership fees, service charges, input cost etc., deposited by individual members. Also, they wanted the well tested SHG route for making all payments for external services so as to maintain transparency.

Results of the Focus Group Discussions in Village Nimsariya, Hoshangabad District, Madhya Pradesh

As a quality assurance measure, Debate, an NGO working with PRIs in Madhya Pradesh was requested to convene focus group meetings with women PRI members and ascertain their reaction to the findings of the Dungarpur survey. Debate organised the focus group meetings in village Nimsariya, Hoshangabad district, Madhya Pradesh.

About Village Nimsariya

The *gram panchayat* Nimasariya has two villages, namely Nimsariya and Dewlakhedi. Nimsariya has a population of more than 4,500 across 1,000 families, whereas Dewlakhedi has 44 families and a population of around 400. The villages have a mix of SC, ST, Muslims and the OBC community.

Agriculture is a major source of livelihood. There are a few large farmers in the village but the rest of the community members have either small or marginal holdings. Soyabean used to be the dominant *kharif* crop. But due to the poor system of disease management, the production dropped. Also, poor prices offered in the market have forced people to shift from soyabean to paddy. Wheat and gram are the other major crops. In the SC and ST communities, most of the households have very small pieces of land and some of the families are landless. Most of these landless families earn their livelihood from wage employment. Agriculture is the biggest source of wage employment available locally. The wage earners get very limited work from the *panchayat*. The village is close to the Basin of River Tawa which is a source of sand that is transported elsewhere. Most of the landless families and families of small and marginal farmers go there as there is prospect of regular work.

The secretary of the *gram panchayat* informed that there is no demand for work under MGNREGS, and in the last two years only ₹ 50,000 has been spent for the construction of a well. In 2011, 14 families were supported under Nandan Falodyan and the total expenditure on this was ₹ 25,000. There are other schemes such as the Mukhyamantri Mazdoor Suraksha Yojna, Indira Awaas Yojana, Mukhyamantri Awas Yojana as well as schemes relating to social security and pension.

The womenfolk in the village work at home and also join men in the field. In the field of agriculture, the division of activities is very clear. Women are not allowed to plough the land but all other activities in agriculture are mainly dependent on them. Recently, harvesters have taken over activities such as cutting and threshing. This has given some relief to the women members of families having land. At the same time, such mechanisation has taken away the opportunity for wage employment from the women folk of landless families. Not all landowners have irrigation facility and depend on those who have wells and pump-sets.

The Group Discussion

Five separate group discussions were organised in village Nimsariya to understand the status of governance, the status of natural resource management and issues related to knowledge and capacity *vis-à-vis the* livelihood needs.

Status of Local Governance in Nimsariya

The *gram panchayat* (GP) is headed by a woman *sarpanch*. Her husband is the Kotwar of the village and the family has 4-5 acres of land. There are 20 ward members in the *gram panchayat* and 10 out of the 20 members are women. Monthly meetings take place regularly and around 8-9 members attend the meetings. But the main demand is for BPL cards and this dominates the discussions. Issues related to health are not discussed.

The services related to the following schemes are under the control of GP:

- Social security pension.
- Wage employment under NREGS.
- Construction of village road.
- Rural housing through IAY and few other schemes.

But the *panchayat* has no influence over services such as supply of drinking water, support for agriculture, services related to energy requirements, distribution of food grains through PDS, services related to health, services related to education and women and child development and support for skill development.

Community members, both men and women feel that the *panchayat* has not been able to identify community-level issues or plan accordingly. The role of the *panchayat* is limited to linking the community with certain selected schemes implemented by the *janpad panchayat* (block level or intermediate-level *panchayat*) and to implementation of selected schemes to be implemented by GP.

Little or No Say in Natural Resource Management

A quick survey of the GPs in all the seven blocks of Hoshangabad district showed that while the responsibility for the management of natural resources lies with the *gram sabha*, with the *panchayats* having the responsibility to work on its direction, in reality the *gram sabha* and the community has little influence on the management of natural resources.

Figure 5.1

Schematic Presentation of Natural Resource Management

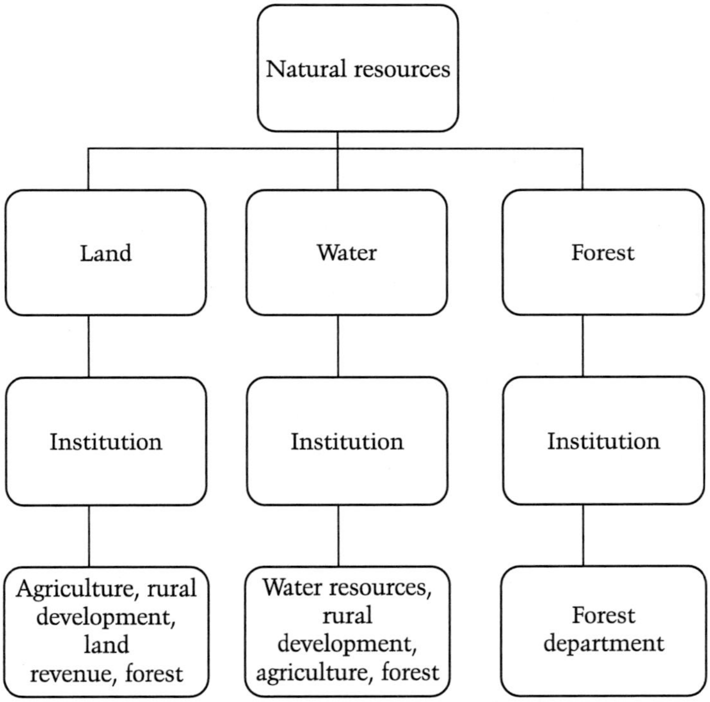

There is no comprehensive plan to mange the natural resources in any of the villages covered in the study. Most of above-mentioned public institutions do not involve *panchayats* in their programmes. Government departments mange natural resources through their own staff and various programmes controlled by them. Only the Rural Development Department works with GP because most of its programmes are directly implemented by *panchayats*. Departments dealing with agriculture, forests, water resources, land revenue and fisheries etc., do not coordinate or work with GPs, and they have poor mechanisms for information sharing with *panchayats* at the intermediate and district level.

Vicious Circle of Knowledge

The women leaders of village Nimsariya stressed that at present, the information flow related to agricultural production and management of natural resources is either absent or limited to the people linked with these departments. The Agriculture Department has some links with one or two big and influential farmers. The Forest Department works through the committee constituted by the department, and the interaction of officials is limited to giving instruction to the president of the committee. The departments concerned with land revenue and irrigation or water resources have no live links with farmers in so far as flow of new information is concerned. The women PRI members mentioned that they have not received any new knowledge from schools or from the government departments. Thus they have to depend on what they have learnt in the field by doing activities and through mutual interaction while working in the field. They suggested that the standing committees of GP and SHGs at the community level need to be used to provide regular information about natural resource management and new scientific practices in the field of agriculture. Also, the self-help system which presently is only linked to mobilisation of cash savings could be useful for enhancing their capacity *vis-à-vis* NRM and farming. For example, new information related to cropping of paddy, could be provided in the following manner:

- Initiating discussion with SHGs before the beginning of the cropping season.
- Preparing a plan for the coming cropping season based on due analysis of the strength and weakness of the farmers and the women's groups.
- Developing a joint strategy of support during the cropping season.
- Organising initiatives to actually provide support during the season. Women PRI members felt that new information will be useful if it is provided at the work site directly.

Strengthening the Role of *Panchayats* in Village Development

The women PRI members suggested the following concrete action plan:

- The *gram panchayat* must acquire the basic information about important programmes.

- At least one or two *panchayat* members should be made responsible for each of the different schemes.
- The *panchayat* members should have the responsibility to coordinate the processes of information flow, planning *vis-à-vis the* scheme and actual support in the field.
- The departments should work through *panchayats*.
- The *panchayats* should work with the ward members and SHGs in the village.
- Skill development is the most important need and *panchayats* must focus on this in coordination with the community and the departments implementing public programmes

Conclusion

The above discussion based on focus group meetings with women PRI leaders in Dungarpur (Rajasthan) and Nimsariya (Madhya Pradesh) shows that participatory governance at the village level is yet at a very rudimentary stage, especially in so far as the role of women PRI leaders is concerned. Yet, there is a clear sign of growing confidence. The women PRI members in Dungarpur stressed that the government will have to make it mandatory for every department to incorporate the suggestions of the village council in every plan. Similar sentiments were expressed in Nimsariya. This growing confidence combined with clarity of vision in women PRI members provides a solid ground for bold steps towards a local livelihood security approach.

6 The Backward Regions Grant Fund (BRGF)

Community Response Towards a Redesign

Overview of BRGF

Several high level Government committees have grappled with the assessment of regional backwardness. In the last year of the Tenth Plan period, the Government of India introduced the Backward Regions Grant Fund (BRGF) with a view to addressing the regional imbalances in development. The Approach Paper to the Twelfth Plan (Planning Commission, 2011) states, 'while the economically-weaker states are catching up in growth rates, there is growing concern about the backwardness of individual districts, several of which are located in States that are otherwise doing well.' Many of these districts are also affected by Left-wing extremism. BRGF and various other regional initiatives have been specially designed to address this problem.

BRGF provides financial resources for supplementing and converging existing developmental inflows into the backward districts so as to:

- Bridge critical gaps in local infrastructure and other development requirements that are not being adequately met through existing inflows.
- Strengthen *panchayat* and municipality-level governance with capacity building support, and facilitate participatory planning, decision-making, implementation and monitoring to reflect local needs.

BRGF has two components namely, a district component covering 250 districts and special plans for Bihar and the districts of Kalahandi, Bolangir and Koraput (KBK) in Orissa.

The starting point for BRGF is a diagnostic study by the district of its backwardness by enlisting professional support. This is to be followed by the preparation of a participatory district development perspective plan to address backwardness. The *panchayats* at the village, intermediate and district level, referred to in Part IX of the Constitution, are expected to undertake planning and implementation of the programme in keeping with the letter and spirit of Article 243 G.

The overall allocation for BRGF for the year 2008-09 was Rs 4,670 crore. The average per capita amount from this development grant varied greatly across the 250 BRGF districts—from less than Rs 81 per capita to between Rs 176 and Rs 3,162 per capita (MoPR website).

World Bank Assessment of BRGF

Some reviews, assessments and concurrent evaluation studies on BRGF are now available. This includes an assessment by the World Bank based on field-visits to eight states (Assam, Andhra Pradesh, Bihar, Chhattisgarh, Madhya Pradesh, Orissa, Rajasthan and West Bengal). This study concludes that BRGF has laid the foundation to achieve several of its specific objectives. BGRF has strengthened local democracy and the roles of the various tiers of the PRI system, and also helped improve vertical coordination and dialogue. By providing *gram panchayats* with some discretionary resources to plan with it has stimulated local participatory planning and improvements in the planning procedures; yet, integrated planning has to be made more effective.

Positive Results

According to the World Bank study, the strength of BRGF is that it is bolstering the basic funding system through provision of discretionary funding to PRIs/ULBs for crucial local investments in public services areas that benefit a large segment of the rural and urban population, and through necessary capacity building (CB) support to PRIs to handle these funds in a proper manner. It is supporting all tiers of the PRI system, through formula-based allocations and a set of guidelines that allow states the necessary flexibility to adjust to local circumstances. The study concludes that this development grant and the CB support have been highly appreciated by stakeholders at different tiers of the government.

The capacity building fund has provided resources for large numbers of training sessions on topics of high relevance for the elected representatives and the officials involved. Innovative CB tools and approaches have been deployed for this purpose.

CB support has contributed to improvements in the governance performance and in the functioning of the entire system of PRIs. It has also contributed to the emerging empowerment of PRIs and communities.

In the eight states combined, over 100,000 local investment projects have been executed within a short period of time. The World Bank report seems to suggest that these projects are generally targeting actual service delivery needs in core local governanace mandates, and in a relatively cost-effective manner. When funds are available, projects are implemented relatively fast (within less than six months) and they are of reasonable quality.

Challenges and Bottlenecks

The World Bank report also brings out the many challenges and bottlenecks in the implementation of BRGF. It concludes that the four stated objectives and the expected outcomes specified in the BRGF guidelines are not clearly defined nor logically structured or linked.

There is a strong need to strengthen various components of the design and operations, if the programme is to achieve the goals of 'mitigating regional imbalances, contributing towards poverty alleviation in backward districts and promote accountable and responsible Panchayats and Municipalities'.

The volume of the BRGF funding remains too small to trigger integrated planning and also too insignificant to generate interest from the line agencies.

The inter-PRI allocations do not usually reflect the variations in needs (and backwardness) and do not take into account factors such as variations in the size of the territories, size of the SC/ST population, number of people below the poverty line, illiteracy rates nor indicators of other expenditure needs.

There are operational weaknesses, and probably one of the most important amongst these is the severe delay in the release of funds. This hampers project execution at all tiers of the local government.

Thus, according to the World Bank report there is need to: i) clarify and improve the investment menu to ensure that it focuses on public investments; ii) ensure that the maximum of 5 per cent allowed for staffing improvements is adhered to; iii) allow for funding of maintenance costs and investment servicing costs within certain ceiling, and iv) improve communication across all tiers about the planning figures, available funds, etc.

The upper tiers of the government need to allow the lower tiers, the necessary discretion to make their own priorities so long as these are within the mandatory functions of the local government, within the prescribed guidelines and in line with the principles of subsidiarity.

Main Recommendations

According to the World Bank report, within the area of planning, the multiple approval steps which delay the adoption of plans by several months every year and compromise PRI autonomy, should be abolished and the entire planning process should be simplified.

The role of the District Planning Committee (DPC) and the High Powered Committee (HPC) should change from that of approval of plans to guidance, coordination and support to the local planning process, and particularly aim to strengthen horizontal coordination and convergence.

There is a need for stronger incentives for the line departments to participate and disclose information about their local investments and activities, and to improve horizontal coordination.

Within the area of capacity building, the delays in implementation and fund underutilisation, as also insufficient coverage of the clients and needs, should be mitigated by: i) a larger degree of outsourcing of CB support, particularly in states with weak State Institute of Rural Development (SIRD), ii) in addition to mandatory, common (supply-driven) CB activities, a gradual move towards a more demand-driven approach whereby PRIs (in the first phase, the *zila parishad*) will become partly in charge of making decisions on the CB initiatives.

To promote synergies and strong incentives for the PRIs/ULBs to improve performance and utilise the CB efficiently, there should be a strong linkage between the regular assessments of the PRI/ULB performance, the capacity building support provided and the size of the development grants.

The present link between the development grant and the CB support should be strengthened as part of a move towards more performance-based funding systems which promote improvements in governance practices and capacity in a systemic manner.

Some of the delays and bottlenecks observed within the operations of BRGF are related to under-sourced and understaffed programme management (PM) arrangements at all tiers of the government. Thus the report contains a number of specific recommendations to boost PM. These include specific proposals to improve the staffing capacity at various levels. The report supports the move to strengthen some of the PM functions at the central and state levels such as IT, data handling, communication and intergovernmental fiscal transfers.

The Report stresses that at the PRI level, the planning and PM functions as well as the social audit functions need further support. Monitoring and evaluation needs to be strengthened through initiatives such as establishment of a baseline for PRI/ULB performance, progress monitoring and concurrent impact evaluation. The report also call for promoting exchange of good practices, peer review mechanisms etc.

The BRGF Plan for Dungarpur (2011-12)

The BRGF plan for Dungarpur for 2011-12 involves an outlay of ₹ 22.54 crore-₹ 20.84 crore for rural areas and ₹ 1.70 crore for urban areas.

The block-wise allocations approved in the BRGF Plan for the district for 2011-12 are as follows:

Table 6.1

Block-wise Allocations Approved in the BRGF Plan for Dungarpur for 2011-12

(₹ *lakh*)

1	*2*	*3*	*4*	*5*	*6*	*7*	*8*	*9*	*10*	*11*	*12*	*13*
Aspur	3.04	5.0	92.0	3.0	14.0	0.0	0.0	16.0	2.0	132.0	4.0	36.0
Bichwada	5.62	5.0	114.5	37.5	0.0	28.1	0.0	49.0	52.5	246.5	6.0	23.0
Dungarpur	3.73	4.0	84.0	33.0	11.0	2.0	0.0	26.0	4.0	158.0	32.0	9.0
Sangwada	3.25	0.0	105.0	0.0	12.0	15.0	6.0	30.0	12.5	109.0	10.0	25.5
Similwada	5.20	5.0	116.0	78.0	6.0	35.0	11.5	48.5	11.0	198.0	8.0	3.0
Total	20.84	19.0	511.5	151.5	43.0	90.0	17.5	169.5	82.0	843.5	60.0	96.5

Notes: 1=Block, 2=Total allocation (Rs lakh), 3=*Kissan Sewa Kendra*, 4=Water pump, 5=*Anganwadi* building, 6=Vetnary hospital, 7=*Patwar* building, 8=*Gram panchayat* building, 9=Community centre building, 10=Drains/small bridges, 11=School rooms, playground, toilets and drinking water in primary and middle schools, 12=Cremation ground, 13=Roads.

As per the planning wing of the district administration, the BRGF Plan has been put together based on proposals received from *sarpanchs*. The capacity building component of BRGF for the state as a whole is sliced-up upfront and placed with the Rajasthan SIRD which then plans and implements various activities designed to build the capacity of elected representatives of PRIs.

It would appear from Table 6.1 that BRGF funds have been allocated in areas that are directly relevant for the needs of the community. However, it would be in order to ask whether or not these add up to a plan that could make a significant difference to the structural factors responsible for endemic backwardness in Dungarpur?

Also, a closer look at the allocation shows that the funds are being utilised mostly for building/construction activities. The capacity building aspect, particularly at the community level is conspicuous by its absence. The feedback on the functioning of BRGF received in the focus group meeting with women PRI leaders throws light on these questions/issues.

Community Response Towards a Redesign of BRGF

The functioning of BRGF was one of the agenda items in the focus group discussion held with 12 women PRI members. The feedback received was startling.

Not a single women PRI member participating in the focus group discussion was aware of the terminology BRGF or of the fact that such a scheme was being implemented in their area. It is thus obvious that none of them had participated in the BRGF planning process. This observation runs quite contrary to the findings of the World Bank review which concluded that BRGF 'has stimulated local participatory planning and improvement in planning procedures as it provides Gram panchayats with some discretionary resources to plan with...BRGF has strengthened local democracy and the roles of the various tiers of the PRI system and helped to improve vertical coordination and dialogue.'

When asked to comment on the appropriates of activities planned under the current BRGF plan for the district, many of the women PRI members responded that the activities listed could be covered under other schemes being implemented by the concerned departments or under MGNREGS. They stressed that BRGF should be utilised for priority activities which can't be covered under other schemes.

The women PRI members outlined the following priorities for BRGF:

- Electrification for agriculture.
- Comprehensive and rigorous training (2-3 times in a year) to female farmers on handling of small agricultural equipment and capacity building of female farmers on agricultural practices in villages, whereas innovative female farmers could be trained in agriculture universities.
- Comprehensive capacity building programme relating to various government schemes.
- Development of village-level seed banks.
- Creation of farm mechanisation centres in villages.
- Establishment of a dairy centre/cooling centre for milk.
- Creation of market infrastructure on cluster basis.
- Establishment of crematoriums.

The women PRI members emphasised that to make BRGF effective, the implementation of the scheme should involve all women PRI members. This is also necessary for ensuring that the benefits reach the poor.

From the above agenda, it is clear that the women PRI members see a much more mainstream role for BRGF in addressing the root causes of backwardness and the sub-optimal livelihood baseline. It is particularly important to note that capacity building of the community in key livelihood areas figures prominently in the list of priorities.

Now, many of the items included in the above agenda cannot be addressed directly under the current structure of BRGF. For example, the vast funds needed in areas such as electrification for agriculture cannot be met out of BRGF. Yet the planning and convergent community mobilisation needs for programmes such as the Rajiv Gandhi Grameen Vidyutikaran Yojana (RGGVY) could certainly be facilitated through BRGF.

Similarly, BRGF could prove to be a vital platform for the proposed community-based agri-extension mechanism since departmentally-driven schemes are not likely to succeed in supporting such an enterprise.

To conclude, there is a need to relocate BRGF from being a small window for discretionary funds and gap filling in local infrastructure to serve as a powerful platform for participatory planning, local capacity building and community-enterprise development under an overarching local livelihood security framework approach.

7 Towards a Local Livelihood Security Framework for Inclusive Development and Inclusive Governance

Introduction

The Eleventh Plan (2007-2012) with its focus on 'faster and more inclusive growth' had set a target for reduction in the poverty ratio by 2 percentage points per year. The Approach Paper to the Twelfth Plan states, 'the Eleventh Plan gave a special impetus to several programmes aimed at building rural and urban infrastructure and providing basic services with the objective of increasing inclusiveness and reducing poverty.' The total cost of the 13 flagship programmes cited in the Approach Paper is estimated at ₹ 691,976 crore during the Eleventh Plan (Planning Commission, 2011).

The results however, show a major slippage *vis-à-vis* the above Eleventh Plan target of poverty reduction. The Approach Paper indicates that according to the preliminary estimates using the latest NSS survey for 2009, the percentage of the population in poverty declined by approximately 1 percentage point per annum during the five-year period 2004-05 to 2009-10. The Approach Paper glosses over this underachievement to the tune of 50 per cent by concluding that while the actual performance was below the target, it was actually better than the results in the earlier decade (i.e., 0.8 percentage points per year during 1993-94 to 2004-05).

What clues emerge from this modest survey in Dungarpur into the factors responsible for the above yawning gap in performance in pro-poor development? What are the messages for the current policy regime which continues to mount one mammoth programme over the other in pursuit of the goal of social security for the poor?

Table 7.1

Expenditure on Flagship Development Programmes over the Eleventh Plan

Sl. No.	*Programme*	*Ministry/Department*	*2007-08 Actual*	*2011-12 BE*	*Total Eleventh Plan*
1	Mahatma Gandhi National Rural Employment Guarantee Act (MGNREGA)	Rural Development	12,661	40,000	156,301
2	Indira Awaas Yojana (IAY)	Rural Development	3,886	10,000	41,486
3	National Social Assitance Programme (NSAP)	Rural Development	3,104	6,158	23,536
4	Pradhan Mantri Gram Sadak Yojana (PMGSY)	Rural Development	6,500	20,000	65,002
5	National Rural Health Mission (NRHM)	Health & Family Welfare	10,509	18,115	69,214
6	Integrated Child Development Services (ICDS)	Women & Child Development	5,193	10,000	38,980
7	Mid-Day Meal (MDM)	School Education & Literacy	5,832	10,380	38,602
8	Sarva Shiksha Abhiyan (SSA)	School Education & Literacy	11,477	21,000	77,576
9	Jawaharlal Nehru National Urban Renewal Mission (JNNURM)	Urban Development	5,508	13,700	48,485
10	Accelerated Irrigation Benefit Programme (AIBP) and Other Water Resources Programme	Water Resources	5,446	12,650	46,622
11	Rajiv Gandhi Gramin Viduyatikaran Yojana (RGGVY)	Power	3,913	6,000	25,913
12	Rajiv Gandhi Drinking Water Mission (Rural Drinking Water)–NRDWP and Total Sanitation Campaign (TSC)	Drinking Water Supply	7,320	11,000	46,722
13	Rashtriya Krishi Vikas Yojana (RKVY)	Agriculture & Cooperation	1,200	7,811	18,550
	Grand Total (after adjusting for others)		81,217	186,539	691,976

Source: Planning Commission, 2011.

The observation that strikes with full force is the innate dynamism and readiness for change at the grassroots even in the context of a remote backward district. The main demands are for participation and partnership towards a productive livelihood base. There is a clear vote for support in areas such as knowledge and assured irrigation over cash subsidy. However, as the survey results show, these very avenues for transformation continue to be the weakest links in the development story.

Overall, the evidence emerging from the Dungarpur survey points to the need for a comprehensive local livelihood security framework to unleash the latent potential at the grassroots. This framework has two main components. First is the immediate priority of a locally relevant extension mechanism. The second, which is also a necessary condition for creating a long-term base for the first, is the broader issue of a strong local governance framework.

Locally-owned Extension Mechanism for Small and Marginal Farmers

As noted in Chapter 2, the agriculture sector in India continues to employ about 55 per cent of the workforce and 80 per cent of all economically active women. The percentage of marginal and small farmers in the total, and also the land operated by them have steadily increased over time. Currently, at the all-India level, they account for more than 80 per cent of all farmers. This stakeholder group is highly vulnerable and lacks access to assets, extension services and production support such as seed, water, credit, subsidy etc. The small and marginal women farmers are particularly vulnerable. Most of them are not recognised as farmers for want of ownership of land and consequently not included as beneficiaries in related government programmes/services.

Bina Agarwal (2010) notes, 'it is well-recognised by policymakers in developing countries that agriculture needs to provide both higher output and viable livelihoods. But the substantial recent focus on infrastructure (irrigation, roads, etc) and research and extension, in countries such as India (see, e.g., the Eleventh Five-Year Plan: GoI 2008) begs the question: by what institutional arrangement will it be ensured that small and marginal and increasingly female farmers have access to the infrastructure? A bottom-up, more collective approach to farming could address these concerns.' Agarwal advances the case for a group approach to overcome the problem of small and fragmented landholdings, and particularly to address the inequity that women farmers face in terms of access to inputs, credit and services. Agarwal notes, 'collective farm activity could range from just joint investment in lumpy (physically indivisible) inputs such as agricultural machinery, to land pooling and joint cultivation by small owners, or even joint land acquisition by purchase or lease. Especially where small and marginal farmers predominate, there could be gains in productivity as well as bargaining power in acting jointly rather than individually. This is likely to be even more the case with women farmers.'

The PPPP Report outlined the need for a robust framework for public-private-community participation in the context of backward districts so as to smoothen out the numerous constraints and bottlenecks that beset not only the supply side but also the demand side (Singh, 2010). The Report presented a PPCP model designed to support tribal families in Dungarpur in achieving an income of over ₹ 25,000 per annum per family on 0.5 ha plots. This PPCP model was developed by CII as a part of its action research project in Dungarpur. The technical details of the above PPCP model are outlined in Annexure A-3.

Box 7.1

CII's Half-Hectare Model: PPCP Strategy

Focus groups meetings with local farmers led to the following conclusions:

- The heavy investment required in the procurement of inputs and equipment is a binding constraint in adoption of new technology. This is particularly true for tribal farmers who do not have any non-agriculture income source apart from seasonal migration as unskilled labour.
- Due to small landholdings, equipment items are not utilised fully. Thus, investment in such items is not economically viable.
- Due to lack of technical know-how, farmers are reluctant to adopt new technologies.
- Overwhelming numbers of farmers are willing to pay for cost-effective provision of services.

Accordingly, CII drew up the blueprint of a model that could help enhance productivity through assured access to irrigation, good quality inputs, farm equipment, credit and agri-extension services. Better returns on agricultural produce were to be achieved through access to agri-markets and marketing infrastructure.

The cropping pattern proposed is based on traditional crops since new crops might entail a cultural barrier. After taking care of the food security needs, the proposed model offers an opportunity for further enhancement in incomes and productivity gains of 30-40 per cent through higher investment in HYV, milch animal(s), horticulture etc.

contd...

...contd...

The strategy proposed for achieving the above objective is to converge public and private investments through private-public-community partnership (PPCP). The PPCP model envisages public investments in augmenting water resources and creating access to water for target farmers, while private investments create various support services in agriculture. Specifically, it is envisaged that public investments would focus on engineering interventions for addressing the gaps in water availability and needs, infrastructure for water conservation, harvesting and recharge, and spatial databases and decision support systems for farmers and communities. Private investments would focus on providing services in areas such as water delivery and irrigation, farm mechanisation, agri-inputs, insurance and risk management, credit access and market linkage.

A special purpose vehicle (SPV) for parking private investments and groups of local semi-literate youth for actually delivering the support services to farmers are important elements of this model.

The institutional mechanism at the community level include water user groups (WUGs) and watershed associations as community-based organisations (CBOs) for governance of water and other natural resources.

Source: Singh (2010).

The PPPP Report suggested a rural service enterprise model building on the above PPCP framework. An overview of the enterprise model may be seen at Annexure A-4.

The findings of the current survey of women farmers in Dungarpur validate some of the parameters of the above PPCP model. For example, the survey shows that the modal landholding amongst the marginal landholders in Dungarpur is around half hectare. Thus, the basic unit underlying the CII's half-hectare PPCP model continues to be valid.

But more important are the valuable clues that the survey provides towards refinement of the institutional framework of the extension mechanism, particularly in so far as the issues of local participation, control and ownership are concerned.

Chapter 5 which outlines the response of women PRI leaders on the contours of a community-based extension mechanism shows that small and marginal women farmers prefer a framework that combines the comfort of small numbers at the cutting edge with the power of large numbers at higher levels where greater negotiation power is required for accessing public resources, facilities and programmes as also for securing a fair deal *vis-à-vis* the suppliers of input and equipment. Most important, the element of mutual cooperation seems to be as vital as the element of collaboration with public agencies and others.

Rather than making a demand for public funding for subsidisation of the said mechanism, the women PRI members take the stand that the funding should come out of membership fees, service charges and input cost deposited by individual members. This underscores the importance of local ownership and control.

As may be seen from Table 4.22 (Chapter 4), knowledge about new farming techniques, about new irrigation techniques, new seeds and inputs emerged as the key requirement for improving farm output. Similarly, the village survey brought out a strong propensity for mutual sharing of equipment, water resources and labour resources at the local community level. Thus, it is not surprising that 86 per cent of the respondents wanted the new support structure to be hosted at the village level (Table 4.35, Chapter 4).

Also, Table 4.36 in Chapter 4, shows that 99 per cent of the respondents in the village level survey reported willingness to pay for maintaining the support services. Similarly, 98 per cent of women farmers showed willingness to pay for requisite mechanisation services, if prices were reasonable and if suitable credit services were made available.

To conclude, both the village survey and the focus group discussions with the women PRI leaders underscore the primacy of a locally-owned and locally-directed extension mechanism and support services.

Refocusing Decentralisation Towards a Locally-owned and Locally-driven Livelihood Security Framework

The buoyancy in the Indian economy over the past decade has had an unforeseen consequence. The rising revenue base of the Central Government in the face of growing political competition as defined by a mosaic of different political parties capturing power in some key states has resulted in a preoccupation with grand centrally-driven social security programmes. Paradoxically, however, the decentralisation momentum which is the natural route to achieving social objectives has got lost in this game of large sums.

Given the above context, the goal of genuine decentralisation has given way to instruments such as 'convergence' of various centrally-driven initiatives and to programmes such as BRGF (which provides a paltry sum of ₹ 20 crore per annum to each backward district for discretionary expenditure) or similar special initiatives for the extremist-ridden areas. The Twelfth Plan Approach Paper continues in a similar vein.

The goal of universal social security and safety net underlying initiatives such as MGNREGS, The Right to Education, The Forest Rights Act and the Food Security Bill is unquestionable to most. However, there is considerable difference of opinion with regard to the modalities for realising such rights. By their very nature, these rights require local empowerment and local solutions. For example, some districts may prefer to achieve the goal of food security by empowering their small and marginal farmers and by implementing the Forest Rights Act in all earnestness. In such a scenario, they may put in only a small and manageable public distribution system (PDS) system to cover the residual population thereby conserving resources for boosting the capacity of farmers and forest dwellers. Solutions such as these may be far more productive and far less costly. The expenditure incurred in this manner is likely to create its matching local supply capacity and will therefore not be inflationary.

The programme for universal food security has reportedly worked well in states such as Tamil Nadu, Orissa and Chhattisgarh. Same is the case for MGNREGA in many fo the states. However, by and large, grand centrally-managed approaches to realising social objectives are likely to be highly costly, corruption-ridden and wasteful. This model has begun to mount tremendous pressure on the fiscal balance and threatens to undermine the economic base of the new resurgent India. This flawed approach is likely to pit the social objectives against the economic objectives—an undesirable trend as these two pillars of social transformation cannot survive and prosper without a symbiotic relationship.

The following paragraphs elucidate the above argument with some concrete examples from the policy space and the policy direction emerging from the Twelfth Plan Approach Paper.

Perils of a Cold 'Convergence Approach'

Consider the Report of the Task Force on Convergence set up by the Ministry of Rural Development around MGNREGA (MoRD/GoI, 2008). This report states,

> substantial public investments are being made for strengthening of the rural economy and the livelihood base of the poor, especially the marginalized groups like SC/STs and women. To effectively address the issue of poverty alleviation, there is need to optimize efforts through inter-sectoral approaches. The convergence of different programmes like, Watershed Programmes, National Agriculture Development Programme (Rashtriya Krishi Vikas Yojana) NADP (RKVY), National Horticulture Mission (NHM), Scheme of Artificial Recharge of Ground Water through Dugwell (ARGW), Accelerated Irrigation Benefit Programme (AIBP), Command Area Development and Water Management Programme (CAD & WM) and Scheme of Repair Renovation and Restoration of Water Bodies (RRR) of Water Resources Department, Backward Region Grant Fund (BRGF), with NREGA will enable better planning and effective investments in rural areas. Convergence also brings synergy between different government programme/schemes in term of planning, process and implementation of programmes/Schemes.

The above bewildering array of schemes with their disparate implementation agencies and approach to decision-making only goes on to show that convergence between them without changing the fundamental logic and structure of local development and governance is a pursuit of the impossible. A simple mapping of the required 'file movement' in various concerned agencies would show the futility of the top-down convergence approach in the context of the existing annual budget cycles.

The Task Force Report displays singular preoccupation with technical expertise. It states, 'to execute the convergence model at the village, block, district level and state level, a technical consortium in consultation with the various departments will be formed. Technical Consortium, which will be suitably strengthened by experts and technical personnel to advise, formulate, appraise and monitor the implementation of the convergence model. The member of technical consortium will be responsible for planning and execution of convergence in a phased manner. The need identification for skill training will also be done by the technical consortium.'

The role of *panchayati raj* has been reduced to that of 'support in decentralised planning (and) value addition in NREGA works'!

Figure 7.1

Technical Consortium

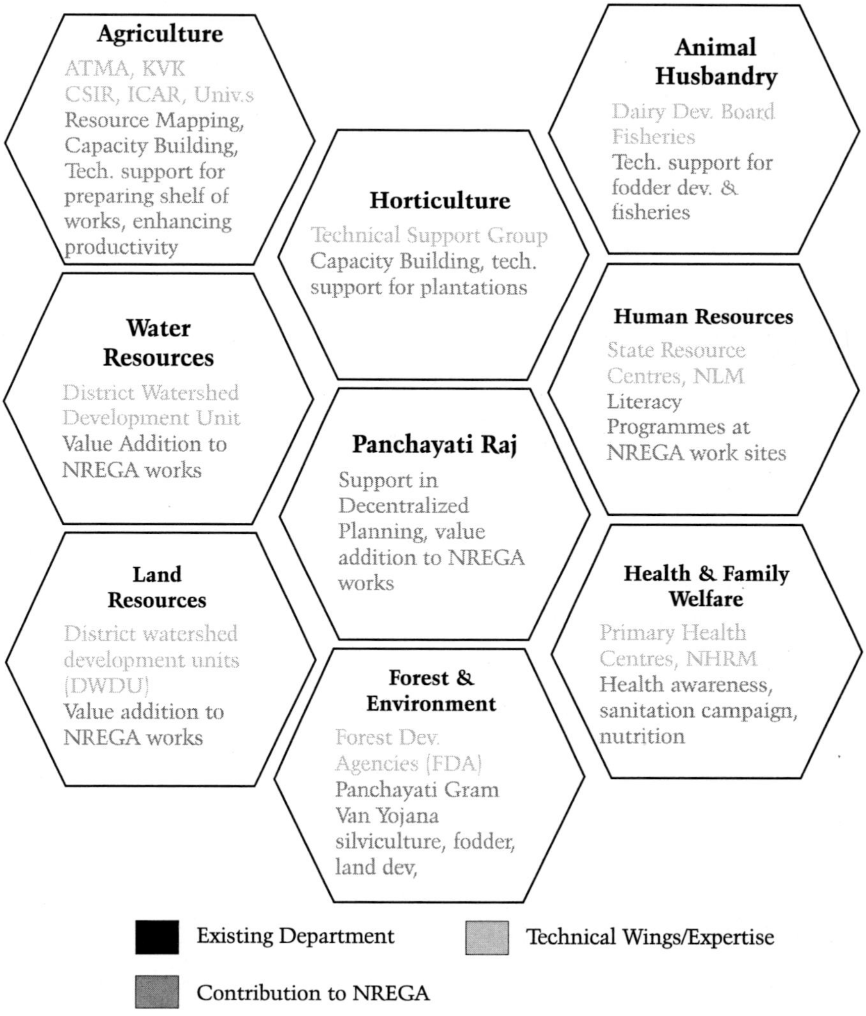

Source: MoRD/GoI (2008).

Similarly, as may be seen from the following flow chart in the Report, it seeks to devolve the leadership role in local planning on to the programme officer for MGNREGA.

S No.	*Action*	*By*	*Due Date*
1.	Convening *gram sabha* for recommendation of shelf of works with priority	Programme officer	By 2nd October of each year.
2.	Receipt of all *gram panchayat* development plans including copy of resolution, recommending the works with priority	---do---	By 3rd week of October
3.	Submission of GPDP of intermediate *panchayat*	---do---	By 3rd week of November
4.	Intermediate *panchayat* approval to the block plan	---do---	Within 15 days of the receipt
5.	Submission of block-wise shelf of projects and the labour budget, to the district *panchayat*.	District programme coordinator	By 3rd week of December
6.	District *panchayat* approval	---do---	By December 31st

Source: MoRD/GoI (2008).

Thus, the proposed convergence schema while appearing sensible on the face of it, is infact an anti-thesis of the spirit of decentralisation and participatory development.

Approach Paper to the Twelfth Plan: Silence on Decentralisation

Preparation of the Approach Paper to the Twelfth Plan should have been an occasion for a fundamental rethink of the pro-poor development strategy (and the underlying inclusive governance models), particularly given its own admission of a 50 per cent slippage *vis-à-vis* the poverty alleviation targets under the Eleventh Plan despite spiralling social sector expenditures (which nonetheless continue to be sub-optimal). But the Approach Paper continues in the same project implementation vein as referred to above. It states,

> As would expect, the effectiveness of their implementation varies from State to State. Instances of misuse of funds are frequently reported in studies and press reports, and these are a legitimate source of concern that needs attention. However, it must be kept in mind that while instances of misuse or leakage present serious problems, they do not necessarily imply that the overall impact of the programme is not positive. For example, Mahatma Gandhi National Rural Employment Guarantee Act (MGNREGA), which

> was started in 2006-07 and extended to cover the whole country during the Eleventh Plan, has seen several instances of misuse of funds, but it has also notched up a remarkable success. It must be admitted, however, that there has been a proliferation of Centrally Sponsored Schemes over a period of years. This has led to poor implementation, duplication, lack of convergence and sub-optimal results.
>
> There is an urgent need to transform the system and sharply reduce the number of schemes. This will enable more focused and effective implementation. A Committee under Shri B.K. Chaturvedi, Member, Planning Commission, has been appointed to review the entire gamut of Centrally Sponsored Schemes and make recommendations for rationalization and consolidation leading to a significant reduction in their number.
>
> With a people-centred, demand-driven architecture, completely different from the earlier rural employment programmes, MGNREGA has directly led to the creation of 987 crore person-days of work since its inception in 2006-07. In financial year 2010-11, MGNREGA provided employment to 5.45 crore households generating 253.68 crore person-days. It has also successfully raised the negotiating power of agricultural labour, resulting in higher agricultural wages, improved economic outcomes leading to reduction in distress migration. This is not to deny that with better project design, implementation leakages could be greatly reduced; and the assets so created could make a larger contribution towards increase in land productivity.
>
> Reforms in implementation of Plan schemes are a priority and should receive focused attention in the Twelfth Plan. There is need for more flexibility in the design of the schemes to reflect the ground realities across the States. Additional provisions should be considered for encouraging innovation; also special efforts to promote convergence at the level of implementation to prevent duplication and to create synergies that improve the quality of outcomes. A detailed assessment of the broad nature of the reforms needed is provided in Chapter 6 (Planning Commission, 2011).

Indeed, Chapter 6 of the Approach Paper focusing on rural transformation has a section on 'Devolution of Powers and Rural Local Self-Governments'. But the section rushes over with this key development theme in three short and insipid paragraphs!

Many of the state governments are taking initiatives towards implementation of the modality of citizen charters. States such as Madhya Pradesh, Bihar, Jammu and Kashmir, Punjab, Delhi, Rajasthan and Goa have taken strides in the direction of Public Service Guarantee Acts (UN Solution Exchange, 2011a). Such measures towards recognising the rights of citizens, timely and efficient delivery of services, enhancing transparency in service provision, holding service providers accountable and bringing citizens closer to the government are a step in the right direction. However, such rights-based instruments will achieve their full transformational potential only if they go beyond some discrete points of government-citizen interface and get aligned to a comprehensive local developmental compact aimed at boosting the local livelihood baseline.

Currently, local developmental programming is highly ad hoc and subject to the exigencies of the budgetary cum approval processes in numerous agencies at the Central/state/district level that provide funds or otherwise partake in the implementation process. This makes it impossible to plan beyond small projects. The study by Krishna and Bajpai (2011) outlined in Chapter 2 shows that developmental impulses have a very short life. They peter out within a distance of 5 kms. Thus, how could one expect the echos of the dins in the *bhawans* of Delhi and the state capitals to reach distant places such as Dungarpur? Endemic poverty in as many as 250 districts in the country is the result of this submergence of local initiative under a massive multi-layered bureaucratic structure. The development machinery which seems to be standing on its head must be put back on its feet in the districts and the blocks.

The concept of a local livelihood security compact would entail a consensus on the key social and economic rights at the national level, but leave the task of their realisation to the district/block level. Thus, locally-elected governments could decide on their own poverty line or 'a minimum living standard guarantee' as is the case under the Dibao programme in China. Such local guarantee frameworks must consistent with the legally binding national standard, but could be pegged higher based on the aspirations of the local citizens. Depending on their unique resource base and vulnerability profile, the local governments could decide on their own strategy mix. Thus for example, Dungarpur may decide to focus its resources on creating 'water security' for its predominantly agricultural population. It may decide to create a village-level food security framework based on successful instances of community grain banks thereby conserving resources for other pressing priorities. Under this approach, the decisions will be local, could be taken quickly and have a strong element of direct accountability. In some other places, more complex solutions may be necessary. For example, in Bihar, where abject landlessness and stunting of rural-urban linkages have together created a vortex of poverty, a programme of 'land reform plus' may be required (Singh, 2012). But again it is clear that the long-term solution to food security does not lie in supplying highly subsidised food to a vast population through PDS.

Box 7.2

Empowering Local Communities to 'Produce Locally-Consume Locally'

(A Contribution to the e-Discussion on the UN Food and Nutrition Community of Practice)

Dear members,

In context of the ongoing discussion on rising food prices, I would like to share my experience from recent visit to the tribal dominated villages of Talai, Rathana and Jharna in Udaipur District of Rajasthan to study the impact of a National Agricultural Innovation Project funded by Indian Council of Agricultural Research (ICAR). The project is implemented by Maharana Pratap University of Agriculture and Technology Udaipur (*http:// mpuat.digitaluniversity.ac/Content.aspx?ID=869*). A self-sustaining model of empowering the local communities to increase income and nutrition through adoption of economically viable integrated farming system models and technologies. Some of the activities include:

- Horticulture and livestock-based integrated farming system modules.
- Basket of technology options.
- Partnership with various agro-input industries.
- Establishment of farm fresh outlet.
- Establishment of rural technology centre in cluster of five villages.
- Sustainability fund creation thorough farmer's contribution to sustain development activities during post-project period.

The transformation of once unreached villages habituated by tribals with bare minimum livelihood availabilities to the present level of awareness is amazing. The changes brought out in food security through horticulture are incredible. Two polyhouses to produce planting materials cater to the planting requirements of the villages. Hybrid sorghum and maize, vegetables like *bhindi*, chilli, cucurbits, tomatoes, onion, fruits like pomegranate, Mango, guava, lemon, papaya are now grown. Ber grafted on

contd...

...contd...

wild beer *in situ* is a notable scientific intervention followed up by tribal farmers.

The assembly of village farmers presented growing standards of health and physique. The mobile technology is making connectivity revolution despite all the handicaps. Base line surveys made four years back and present surveys indicate reasonably good impact of the NAIP.

Empowering local communities to 'produce locally-consume locally' as indicated in Anushuman's response would be key to cope with situations of rising food prices rather than depending on subsidies and external support.

Investment in infrastructure, marketing systems, extension and communication services, education, as well as in research and development, can increase food supply and improve the functioning of local agricultural markets, resulting in less volatile prices. In this way, markets can work for the poor people who bear the burden of food price volatility.

—K.V. Peter, World Noni Research Foundation, Chennai.

Source: UN Solution Exchange (2011b).

The charter outlined by women PRI leaders in Section 5 focuses on year-round availability of clean drinking water, quality education in villages and resolution of issues relating to agriculture with major focus on the availability of irrigation to all and on the supply of quality agri-inputs. This charter also lays emphasis on discussing thoroughly during *panchayat* general meetings, every activity/scheme proposed to be implemented in the village and incorporating genuine issues related to village development without any bias. Their agenda for BRGF outlined in Section 6 is consistent with the above matrix.

This charter provides assurance that strengthening the mechanisms for local direction will make poverty vanish far more quickly than ever imagined in exercises such as MDG target setting.

Broader Linkages for Local Compact

While public extension services in the agricultural sector have not kept pace with new challenges and opportunities, a number of business agencies have built up impressive capacities and networks in input supply and extension services. Such capacities include many other areas that are of direct relevance to the *aam admi* in poorest districts. Examples are safe drinking water, water prospecting, irrigation, conservation and value addition to agricultural products, use of ICT in education and health services, a host of financial services etc.

The poorer areas and sections of the population, however, continue to remain unserved by wider economic forces and institutions. This is because the transaction costs of engagement in any activity beyond direct buying and selling of commodities remain enormously high. Such high transaction costs arise not only because of weak physical infrastructure, but also on account of restrictive rules combined with large grey areas where taking any partnership initiative requires long, cumbersome and costly efforts at breaking new grounds. Thus, even where such partnerships take place, business firms focus on deriving high short-term returns consistent with the high risks and uncertainties. Often the firms use their superior bargaining power to pass on the risks to the weaker local players.

Thus, instead of pursuing elusive goals such as 'convergence' between vertical public programmes through mechanisms such as technical consortia, the government should focus on addressing the core issues and institutional bottlenecks responsible for the enormously high transaction costs and on creating nimble and workable legal modalities for partnership between local communities, the business sector and public agencies. The current reliance on voluntary corporate social responsibility type approach must give way to a more formal legal and institutional framework which carries both carrots and sticks. Similarly, the rules of engagement with public agencies must move towards a system of legally binding compact.

The most vital link in this chain is the strengthening of community capacity. This includes issues such as property rights for the poor, both for the assets held individually and for community resources. Without clear property rights, local actors will not be able to partner with the organised sector, nor can they muster resources such as credit to join new ventures.

MGNREGA was a bold, courageous and unconventional response to a stark social reality. But the next logical step towards broadening the charter of social and economic rights lies not in heaping more of the same.

The Twelfth Plan Approach Paper started on a bullish note citing the strong macro fundamentals of the Indian economy in its opening sentence.

The sharp downturn in 2011 forewarns against the perils of papering over structural issues by flashing large sums of money. It is a timely reminder for reviving and resurrecting a genuine initiative in the area of decentralisation. The evidence from this modest survey of small and marginal women farmers in Dungarpur promises a ready ground for a giant leap in inclusive development and inclusive governance.

Annexures

Annexure A-1

The ToR for the Study

The ToR of this study includes:

- A survey covering eight villages in Dungarpur to identify from the point of view of small and marginal women farmers, the matrix of interaction between NRM and livelihoods on the one hand, and the existing empowerment framework on the other.
- Analysis of the design and implementation of public policies and programmes in the light of the above matrix. The former includes interventions such as the Backward Regions Grant Fund (BRGF).
- Review of the local governance framework, again in the light of the matrix referred to above.
- Recommendations on: (a) mechanisms for breaking the vicious cycle in knowledge, resources and capacity deprivation that women face in a depleting natural resource base scenario. (b) The contours of the self-help mechanism required for meeting the needs in the above areas (i.e., knowledge, resources and capacity). (c) How grassroots women leaders could adopt modern scientific planning tools to break the above vicious cycle? (d) The role that public programmes need to play in targetting the above 'soft' factors that are at the base of persistent gender inequity, low productivity from the natural resource base and the resultant endemic poverty.

Annexure A-2

CII's Dungarpur PPCP Model

1. Brief profile of various pilot activities undertaken by CII in Dungarpur

CII has been involved in various pilots and ground-level activities in Dungarpur for last four years or so. This includes participatory crop demonstration trials, development of WUGs and undertaking investments in water management systems for WUGs activities. This experience has enabled development of a PPP-based agri-business development model.

Table A-2.1

Profile of CII Engagement with Local Communities in Dungarpur

Sr. No	*Particulars*	*Total*
1	Village profiles	
	Total number of villages	34
	Villages of canal command areas	24
	Villages of rainfed areas	10
	Geographical area of 34 villages (in ha)	20,772
	Cultivable area of 34 villages (in ha)	10,970
	Irrigated area of 34 villages (ha)	3,494
2	Water user groups	13
	WUGs in rainfed areas	11
	WUGs in tail end areas of canal command	2
	Total WUG members	169
	Total land of 13 WUGs (in ha)	85.3
3	Agriculture profile	
	Crop cultivated: *kharif*	Maize, *urad*, *tuar*, soyabean, paddy
	• *Rabi*	wheat, barley, chick pea, mustard
	• Summer	*moong*
4	Agriculture-based intervention	
	No. of seasons of intervention	1. *Kharif* : 2 2. *Rabi* : 3 3. Summer : 2
	Crop trials conducted, 0.2 ha each.	1,388 nos.
	No. of farmers involved: *kharif*	1. Maize: 315 2. *Urad*: 111 3. Soyabean: 46
	No. of farmers involved: *Rabi*	1. Wheat : 416 2. Barley: 168 3. Chick pea : 214 4. Mustard : 17
	No. of farmers involved: Summer	1. *Moong* : 113

In Dungarpur, designated under Udaipur Agro Climatic Zone–IV B, CII and partnering organisations have been involved in crop demonstration trials in participatory mode for last over three years. Highlights of the results are presented in the following table.

Table A-2.2

Results of Crop Productivity Trials in Dungarpur

Sr. No.	*Crops*	*Productivity Level, qt/ha*			
		Rainfed Scenario		*Canal Irrigated Scenario*	
		Avg. qt (per ha)	*Max. qt (per ha)*	*Avg. qt (per ha)*	*Max. qt (per ha)*
1	Maize	Kaveri-235 - 37	66	PHEM-2 - 38	47
2	*Urad*	T-9 - 11	15	-	-
3	Soyabean	-	-	JS - 335 - 8	11
				Pratap Soya -1 - 15	22
4	Wheat	Lok-1 - 38	45	39	56
5	Barley	-	-	RD 2035 - 38	50
6	Mustard	BIO - 902 - 12	15	-	-
7	Chick pea	ICCC-37 - 12	15	Dahod Yellow - 12.5	15
		KAK - 2 - 10	12	-	-
8	Summer *moong*	-	-	K-851 - 8	10

Note: A price difference of about 35 per cent was observed when deficient micronutrients applied through combined commercial products available in market over micronutrients applied through compounds such as boron through borax, sulphur through gypsum, zinc through zinc sulphate.

High value crops cultivation has been taken up with farmers on pilot basis. Details of this pilot activity are given below. Since local farmers are not familiar with such crops; this activity was taken up on a limited basis to demonstrate the benefits of high value cultivation.

Table A-2.3

Profile of Pilot Initiative to Promote High Value Crops

Sr. No.	*Activity*	*Implications*
1	Area coverage	10 ha
2	No. of farmers	45
3	Productivity per ha	13 tonne
4	Costs benefit ratio	Avg. 1:7

The key to the success of the proposed initiative is building institutions with robust charters that are acceptable to the local communities. Under Farmers

Participatory Action Research Programme (FPARP), 13 WUGs were formed in both rainfed as well as tail end areas of canal command. The average investment requirements on water resource development and water management systems are given below:

Table A-2.4

Average Investments on Water Resource Development and Management for WUGs

Sr. No.	*Activity*	*Output*	*Cost implications*
1	Water conservation	1. Farm bundings for in situ moisture conservation (1,000 running meter). 2. One earthen check dam. 3. Loose stone check dams (482m3). 4. Drainage network in canal command areas to bring additional land under cultivation (1.2 X 2 X 2,500 mt).	1. Avg. Rs 0.40 lakh on water conservation per group. 2. Rs 1.25 lakh on drainage network.
2	Hydrogeological study and resource mapping	1. Hydrogeological study to identify recharge and discharge areas for WUGs. 2. Micro planning and resource mapping of village resources (10 villages). 3. Creation of thematic maps of village resources.	1. Avg. Rs 0.20 lakh per group for hydrogeological study. 2. Avg. 0.30 lakh per village on micro planning.
3	Water source development	1. Developed three Fresh wells. 2. Developed eight existing wells. 3. Two wells are already developed.	1. Avg. Rs 1.00 lakh for fresh well. 2. Avg. Rs 0.6 lakh for existing well.
3	Water pumping and distribution system per group.	1. Seven DG set with electric motor and 540 mt pipeline with 15 sprinkler nozzles per group. 2. Two electric motors with 360 mt pipeline and 10 nozzles.	1. Rs 1.25 lakh on DG and pumping and distribution system per group. 2. Rs 0.65 lakh on pumping and distribution system only.

Note: Avgerage 60-70 per cent water saving over traditional method was observed per irrigation using sprinkler irrigation techniques.

Effort has been made to promote weather insurance for risk coverage. The investment costs for providing this service and other details are given later on.

Table A-2.5

Cost Implications of Providing Customised Weather Insurance

Sr. No.	*Activity*	*Implications*
1	Private investment (per 225 sq. km area)	Avg. ₹ 2 lakh on two automatic weather stations.
2	Total farmers benefitted during *rabi* 2008-09 season.	174 nos.
3	Total area covered in pilot activity.	131 ha
4	Crops covered and premium amount	Chick pea: 23 ha & Wheat: 108 ha

IEC plays an important role in providing extension and information services to farmers. A mobile IT van called 'grameen Vikas Rath' equipped with audio visual aids, internet connectivity was arranged to provide IEC services to farmers.

2. The Half-Hectare Model

The experience gained by CII over the last few years has helped in evolving a model that could enable poorly endowed tribal families to achieve an income of over Rs 25,000 per annum per family on 0.5 ha plots through enhanced agricultural productivities and better returns on agricultural produce. The target families are poorly endowed tribal families who do not have dependable access to water, good quality agri-inputs, investment funds, extension services and markets. The proposed cropping pattern at this stage is based on traditional crops since new crops might entail a cultural barrier.

2A. Techno-Economic Details of the Proposed Half-Hectare Model

The techno-economic details of the proposed half-hectare model are as follows:

Table A-2.6

Land Use, Productivity, Production, Market Rates and Gross Income

Season	*Crop$*	*Area, (ha)*	*Productivity# (qt/ha)*	*Production (qt.)*	*Market Rate (₹/qt.)*	*Gross Income (₹)*
Kharif	Maize	0.375	36	13.5	800	10,800
	Paddy	0.125	30	3.75	1000	3,750
Rabi	Wheat	0.4	39	15.60	1200	18,720
	Chick pea	0.1	12	1.2	1960	2,352
Summer	*Moong*	0.25	8	2	3400	6,800
	Crop residue@			65.7	150	9,855
All	Summary	0.5		34.55	34.55	52,277

Notes: # Productivities can further rise by 30-40 per cent.
@ Crop residue can be used as fodder for maintaining HYV milch animals.
$ It is possible to plant horticultural plants on farm bunds.

Table A-2.7

Expenditures and Net Incomes for 0.5 Hectare Model

(in ₹ '000)

Activity	*Rainy Season*	*Winter*	*Summer*	*Total*
Agri input	1.7875	3.24	0.575	5.6025
Insurance	0.14	0.19	0	0.33
Water charge				
Pump and distribution system + power generation	1.152	2.37	0.86	4.382
Mechanisation				
(ploughing, harrowing, puddling, sowing, transplanting, harvesting by reaper, paddy thresher, multicrop thresher)	1.00	1.27	1.04	3.31
Total	4.0795	7.09	2.475	13.625
Provision for bank charges				12.00#
Projected gross income				52.277
Projected net income				26.652

Note: # This will cover EMI on bank loans for term investments that will be added to services charges, as well as microfinance to farmers for annual working capital.

Table A-2.8

Present Expenditures and Incomes on 0.5 ha: Irrigated and Unirrigated Conditions

(in ₹ '000)

Activity	*Per 0.5 ha per Year under Rainfed Condition*	*Per 0.5 ha per Year under Irrigated Condition*
Avg. cost of agri inputs	0.55	2.3
Insurance	0.125	0.25
Mechanisation	0.70	1.70
Water charge	0.50	4.05
Total expenditure	1.875	8.30
Gross income including fodder	12.75	35.00
Net income	10.875	26.7

Note: Insurance was provided by LAMPS and only covers crop insurance.

WUGs are proposed to be formed on 30-50 ha small watersheds on second/third order streams. Each such small watershed may contain about 10-15 farmers and about 7 ha agricultural land will be targetted for the proposed cropping pattern and proposed support services. The water balance of the 30-50 ha watersheds will be as follows.

2B. Water Management Model

A suitable approach to water management is at the core of the half-hectare model. The main elements of the proposed water management model are as follows:

Table A-2.9

Water Requirements of the 0.5 Hectare Model
Irrigation Water requirement (1 Irrigation = 900 m³)

Sr. No.	*Crop*	*Season*	*No. of Irrigations, (Nos.)*	*Water Application (m^3 /ha)*	*Water Requirement as per 0.5 ha Model (m^3)*
1	Maize/paddy/ *urad*/soyabean	*Kharif*	2	1800	900
2	Wheat/barley	*Rabi*	5	4500	1800
3	Chick pea/mustard	*Rabi*	2	1800	180
4	*Moong*	Summer	3	2700	675
	Total				3555

Table A-2.10

Water Balance for a 40 Hectare Watershed

Particulars	*Water Balance for 40 ha Watershed at Break-even Rainfall 489 (82 per cent ependability)*
Total rainfall volume ('000'cum)	195.6
Various losses @ 20%	39.12
In-situ water use of cultivable land ('000' cum)	14
In-situ water use of forest and pasture lands ('000' cum)	34
Effective runoff volume after 20% further losses ('000'cum)	108.48
Total applied irrigation for 14 households	49.77
Balance water ('000' cum)	58.71
Irrigation as % of effective run-off	46%
Irrigation as % of rainfall	26%

Table A-2.11

Investment Requirements for Water Resource Development and Management

(in ₹ '000)

Activity	*One Time Investment*	*Operating Cost/0.5 ha*	*Investment Cost/0.5 ha*	*Remark*
Public investment for water resource development in a small 30-50 ha watershed on second – third order streams.				
Creation of common water resource for WUG.	240.00		17.10	Two wells for each group
Water conservation for enhancement of groundwater potential in vicinity of common water resource.	600.00		43.00	For a small 30-50 ha watershed on second-third order stream
Sub Total	840.00		60.10	
Bankable investment for agriculture on 7 ha agri area in the small watershed.				
Pumps and distribution system	72.00	*Kharif*: 0.352 *Rabi*: 0.77 Summer: 0.26 Total: 1.382	5.15	A group of 7 ha agri area is considered.
Power generation unit, 7.5KVA for group	56.00	*Kharif*: 0.8 *Rabi*: 1.6 Summer: 0.6 Total: 3.00	4.00	Due to lack of power grid connectivity
Sub Total	128.00	4.382	9.15	
Total	968.00	4.382	69.25	

2C. *Inputs Costs for 0.5 Hectare Model*

The details of the input costs are as follows:

Table A-2.12

Inputs Costs for 0.5 Hectare Model

(in ₹ '000)

Input Service	*Crop Input Cost for 0.5 Hecatre Model*				
	Maize	*Paddy*	*Wheat*	*Gram*	*Moong*
(Area in ha)	(0.375)	(0.125)	(0.40)	(0.10)	(0.25)
Seed	0.45	0.10	1.00	0.40	0.225
Fertiliser	0.6375	0.175	0.72	0.12	0.10
Pest	0	0.025	0.08	0.02	0.05
Micro nutrient	0.30	0.10	0.32	0.08	0.20
Total cost of input per ha	1.3875	0.40	2.52	0.72	0.575

Note: Season-wise inputs costs in Rs '000/-: *Kharif* = 1.7875; *Rabi* = 3.24; Summer = 0.575.

2D. *Cost of Farm Mechanisation Services*

One set of farm equipment, as described below is planned for two villages covering 14 WUG, 7 per each village, and total agricultural land of about 100 ha, 7 ha per group and 50 ha per village.

Table A-2.13

Costing for Farm Mechanisation Services

(in ₹ '000)

Mechanisation	*Tractor*	*Plough*	*Harrow*	*Cage Wheel*	*Seed Drill*	*Paddy Thresher*	*Multi Crop Thresher*	*Paddy Trans-planter*	*Reaper*
One time investment	4.500	0.450	0.200	0.500	0.400	0.450	0.800	0.800	0.600
Operating cost per year	0.788	1.159	1.237	1.233	0.544	1.605	1.812	0.630	0.727
Operating cost per ha		0.012	0.004	0.008	0.005	0.013	0.01	0.007	0.007
Season-wise operating cost for 0.5 hectare model									
Kharif			0.21	0.10		0.09	0.36	0.16	0.08
Rabi			0.21		0.24		0.48		0.34
Summer		0.58	0.10		0.12		0.24		
Total		0.58	0.52	0.10	0.36	0.09	1.08	0.16	0.42

Note: Season-wise total operating costs for 0.5 ha model: *Kharif* = 1.0; *Rabi* = 1.27; Summer = 1.04. Total annual operating costs for 0.5 ha model = 3.31.

2E. Total Investment Costs

This includes investments on water management and farm mechanisation equipment as well as working capital requirements of farmers.

Table A-2.14

Average Term Investments on Equipment (for 0.5 Hectare and for each WUG)

(in ₹ '000)

	Summary of Bankable Investment Cost		
	Requirements for 0.5 ha Model	*Requirements per WUG, i.e., 7 ha*	*Requirements for 525 WUG*
Pumps and distribution	5.143	72.00	37,800
Power generation	4.00	56.00	29,400
Mechanisation			
Avg. machinery cost, initial investment	4.436	62.10	32,602.5
Total	13.579	190.10	99,802.5 Or Approx. Rs 10 crore

Working capital requirements of farmers are as per tables above, covering costs of inputs, insurance, water services and farm mechanisation services for 0.5 ha in ₹ '000 = 13.645.

Therefore, total credit requirement for 0.5 ha in ₹ '000 = 27.224

Therefore, the provision of ₹ 12,000 per 0.5 ha towards bank charges is sufficient even for high interest rate for shorter duration loans. There is an in-built cushion for unexpected losses.

The total potential for engagement with banks for 525 groups=approx. ₹ 20 crore.

2F. Estimation of the Minimum Scale Required for the Social and Economic Viability of the Proposed Model

The scale estimation is based on the assumption of generating agricultural surplus equivalent to 50 per cent of trade volume required for viable agri-business of corporates. The targeted surplus is generated after accounting for the food security requirements of the farmers.

Table A-2.15

Estimation of Minimum Scale Required for the Social and Economic Viability of the Proposed Model

Crop	*Maize*	*Paddy*	*Wheat*	*Moong*	*Chick Pea*
Food requirement, qts. per person per year	1.10	0.21	1.30	0.08	0.13
Total family food requirement, qts. per year (avg. size 3 adults + 2 children)	5.50	1.05	6.50	0.40	0.65
Total food grain production, qt.	13.5	3.75	15.6	2	1.2
Marketable surplus per household, qt.	8	2.7	9.1	1.6	0.55
Marketable surplus per group, MT	11.2	3.78	12.74	2.24	0.77
Marketable surplus target for viable business, MT	10000	3500	10000	2000	700
Marketable surplus target for WUGs, MT	5000	1750	5000	1000	350
Groups required to produce targetted production	447	463	393	447	455
No. of villages required to be covered for developing 500 groups	72. Therefore, say 75				
Total revenue area required to be covered for 75 villages	33,750 ha				
Total watershed area required to be covered	37,500 ha (say 35,000 to 40,000 ha)				

ANNEXURE A-3

Towards an Organised PPPP-based Rural Service Enterprise Model

1. The Need for a Robust Local Development Framework

The poor state of public extension services has been highlighted in public reports including the plan working group reports of the Planning Commission. Large public funding has flowed towards creation of an elaborate agricultural extension infrastructure. However, the infrastructure created has not kept pace with the changing needs. Assets created are languishing as operational expenses dry up based on changing plan schemes. Field visits during this study confirmed that this was the ground-level reality in Sawaimadhopur in Rajasthan, Almorah in Uttarakhand, and surprisingly also in the agriculturally well-off area in Ladwa in Karnal, Haryana.

Box 1

The Changing Needs of Farmers for Support from Agricultural Extension

The performance of public sector extension is under scrutiny for quite some time and questions are being raised on its capability to deliver goods in the rapidly changing environment. The shifting emphasis of Indian agriculture towards diversification, commercialisation, sustainability and efficiency has made it necessary for the state extension organisations to critically examine their extension approaches.

Liberalisation of agricultural trade consequent to the WTO agreements has resulted in new opportunities and threats to Indian agriculture. India is likely to gain in some crops, but consistent efforts for improving quality (to meet international standards) and increasing cost-effectiveness (increasing productivity, achieving cost reduction) in these crops/products are essential to achieve these. Liberalisation of agricultural imports, which would gain further momentum in the months to come, would subject our producers to competition from outside. There is an urgent need to increase the competitiveness of Indian agro-products.

Public investments in agriculture, (investments in irrigation, rural roads, rural electrification, storage, marketing, agricultural research and education, land development, co-operation etc,) in real terms since mid-seventies have been declining consistently in all the States. Farmers have to join together to put pressure on governments to invest more and have to pool together their resources to develop and maintain the necessary infrastructure. Extension may have to support farmers in this endeavour.

Due to changing face of agriculture, farmers have to make a number of complex decisions now. To make good decisions, farmers need information from different sources and often need help to integrate them.

contd...

...contd...

Many new institutions (private and public) that have emerged during the last two decades are found to be providing support to farmers in some of the above areas. However, "their concentration of manpower and expenditure in specific crops and regions are affecting their effective outreach to the masses." Moreover, it is difficult to replicate them on a wider scale. The performance of the public sector extension agencies in either meeting many of the above needs or in integrating information from different sources have not been satisfactory. To perform these roles effectively, the DoA need more diverse types of expertise than what is available at present.'

'As discussed earlier, the role of agricultural extension in the next decade should be quite different from what it was 10 years ago or even now. Its role as a facilitator of agricultural knowledge system would only increase as more participants from private sector would get involved in extension. It is likely that input related extension (seed, fertiliser, machines and chemicals) would move to private sector in the future. The public sector extension would still continue to be the major extension provider in most parts of the country as the private sector alone would not be able to meet even partially the varied needs of farmers. The ability of the system to perform these roles would entirely depend on the pace of internal reforms, the system would undergo. Experience the world over is that it is easy to change farmers than to change government agencies. Internal reforms are thus going to be the greatest challenge for the Indian Extension System.

Source: Extracts from the article by Sulaiman (2000).

The report of the Working Group on Gender Issues, Panchayati Raj Institutions, Public Private Partnership, Innovative Finance and Micro-finance in Agriculture for the Eleventh Five Year Plan (2007–2012) observed, 'agricultural extension by government is almost non-existent at village level because government has less staff and its focus is mainly on subsidy schemes... As a result, private traders enjoy oligopolies in supply of seeds and other inputs on credit. This results in exploitation of poor farmers on the one hand and their poor information base on the other hand. PRIs play almost no role here. There is a need to change this situation by involving PRIs and NGOs (CBOs) in this task.' It adds, 'in this context we recommend (1) to appoint village youths as para-workers for agricultural extension. They will be accountable to villagers through PRIs and (2) to provide a legal framework for input supply through institutions like PRIs, SHG federations, private traders and farmer's organisations. PRIs can play this important role as a Governance body. It can promote a Sub Committee for agriculture, which can link cooperatives, CBOs and user groups. Gram Sabha can select Agri Para Workers and make them accountable to it by organizing their payment through Gram Panchayats. Also, licence for input supply can be given to sub committee for Agriculture (under

PRIs) and SHGs along with cooperatives. AKRSP (I) has developed this model in Gujarat and this needs to be replicated after a careful review.'

The working group thus outlines an alternate rural service model. This model while projecting an important role for PRIs, seems to reject the private sector.

Based on the evidence gathered through field visits, consultation with stakeholders, and literature review, this study concludes that the above model needs modification on several counts. First, in most states, PRIs do not have the requisite capacity or the institutional support to be able to handle the kind of management tasks envisaged by the working group. Second, the above model may draw PRIs deep into commercial transactions. This may detract from its governance mandate. Available evidence points to serious risks in this approach. Third, the above model ignores completely the current reality that well established brands are entering agriculture and allied sectors, not only for supply of inputs, but to also provide a host of supplementary services. Their entry is important for containing the rampant counterfeit market in agricultural inputs. Fourth, the above model outlines only the delivery aspects at the field level. But both extension and input supply have much broader dimensions that need to be factored in. For example, how should the public assets lying with government extension agencies be best utilised? What is the best modality for utilising the current public funding for extension services? In other words, a broader systemic solution for extension services is called for.

This report suggests an orgainsed PPPP-based rural service enterprise model. The following evidence from the case studies in the report supports the above approach:

- The weakness in the public agricultural extension machinery is all pervasive. It is stunting both local productivity and value addition opportunities.
- PRIs have a very limited role in agriculture and related areas. This may be impacting both the agricultural sector as well as PRI's own place in the rural economy.
- PPCP models that ensure to each tribal family, an income of over Rs 25,000 per annum on 0.5 ha plots even in the context of a highly hostile eco-environment are feasible.
- The role of the private sector cannot be substituted by NGOs or any other implementing agency.
- There is a realisation in the business sector that their profits could improve through deeper engagement in the backward linkage chain and that PRI members could be an important ally in an organised effort in this direction.

- PPPP projects are likely to fail if they are handled like any other departmental programme. Thus, a new organisational framework for local development is required to promote PPPP initiatives on the desired scale.
- The importance of even simple platforms for partnerships in generating ideas and opportunities-platform for a dialogue between the PRI members themselves, as well as for interaction with other stakeholders.

2. PPPP-based Rural Service Enterprise Model

In the context of this short study, it is difficult to define in any depth, the shape that an organised PPPP-based rural service enterprise model would take. However, some broad direction is presented below.

First, a SPV needs to be created to consolidate public assets (particularly, the field-level assets) relevant for extension services in agriculture and allied sectors and make them available for the delivery of such services by the most competent agency selected on a competitive basis.

The SPV could be at the state level, but there could be a strong case for creating the SPV at the district level as the latter may be in conformity with the PRI mandate. There could be further stratification depending on the scale to be adopted for contracting out extension services. For example, if after due consideration, the development block is considered to be the most appropriate or feasible unit for contracting out extension services, the SPV model should facilitate such contracting.

Second, a good portion of the existing public funding for agricultural extension (and a number of related services) needs to be pooled in and channelled through the above mechanism to enable universal provision of a basic menu of extension services (e.g., soil mapping, pre-harvesting advice at the micro level, disease surveillance and guidance, weather forecasts and local implications, certain minimum post-harvesting guidance etc.). The use of public assets (discussed above) as a part of the contract should help drive considerable economy.

Third, to draw-in the best agencies for supply of such services, the implementing agency should be selected on an open–quote basis. The net should be cast wide and public agencies, private agencies, NGOs, cooperatives, etc., who qualify certain eligibility criteria should be allowed to bid.

Fourth, the contract should be for a period long enough to enable the selected agencies to make complimentary investments and recoup them through provision of value added services.

The PRIs would have a dual role in the above model. It would establish a two-way interaction with extension agency in the context of local planning. This would help promote convergence of development activities at the local level. The PRI would also be responsible for monitoring delivery of services by the extension agency. For this function, suitable participatory mechanisms need to be created within the PRI to minimise the chances of corruption in certification of compliance. These functions would also provide a good window for strengthening the resource base of PRIs.

In this model, the government machinery could focus on planning and implementation of investment activities to stem the declining trend of public investment in agriculture. If taken up in all earnestness, this could absorb a lot of staff to be redeployed. Further, public agencies and government servants could potentially play a useful role in the new extension framework itself. As insiders to the larger government machinery, they can coordinate some of the tasks relatively more easily. Attracted by opportunities for local postings, some may opt to move over to the SPV on a tenure deputation basis provided the security of tenure and service conditions as government employees are not adversely affected.

There is a potential risk of the small and marginal farmers being excluded under the proposed framework. But evidence that leads to contra conclusions also exists. While individually, the small and marginal farmers are weak, as a group they have significant economic strength. Eighty-eight per cent of small farmers own almost 50 per cent of cultivated land and more than 50 per cent of irrigated area. They reportedly lease in more than 30 per cent cultivated land (mostly irrigated). Fertiliser consumption per unit area by small farmers is significantly higher than the rest. Some firms in the input supply business report that small farmers are no more subsistence producers but actually are surplus producers and technology transfer at their farms is better compared to others. Thus, it is not surprising that institutional innovations are taking place to cater to the needs of the small farmers. For example, Tata Chemicals Limited is organising a Producer Company (PC) for small vegetable growers in Punjab.

Another risk in this model is the possible conflict of interest if the contract is awarded to an existing input supplier. The firm may use this opportunity to push its own products. Instituting mechanisms and measures to avoid or mitigate such conflict of interest and to ensure a level paying field for others would be one of the serious challenges in operationalising the new system.

The above organised PPPP model calls for an enhanced public responsibility for rural livelihoods rather than a dilution in such responsibility. But as discussed above, in place of the traditional development approaches based on the monopoly of government implementation of all public programmes, it calls for new role allocation based on respective mandates and capacities.

3. Concluding Remarks

This report suggests creation of a new PPPP-based rural service enterprise model. But in most states, these are precisely the set of issues that have been most difficult to come to grips with. Thus, is this idea an impossible or impracticable proposition to start with?

Some great success stories in the cooperative domain, the runaway success of the telcom revolution and other experiments based on the BoP paradigm as well as breakthrough in the challenging social sectors (e.g. the Yashaswini Health Insurance Scheme with over 4.0 million enrollments in a short span of time) lend hope. Admittedly, while the rural service enterprise model would be far more complex, a number of sub-systems of such an approach are already proven. The time is ripe for experimenting with organisational models suited to the administrative systems and traditions as well as the character of local social capital in different states/regions.

References

Agarwal, Bina (2010). "Rethinking Agricultural Production Collectivities", *Economic & Political Weekly* XLV(9). February 27.

Bardhan, Pranab (2010). *Awakening Giants: Feet of Clay*. Princeton NJ: Princeton University Press.

Dabholkar, S.A. (1998). *Plenty for All: Prayog Parivar Methodology*. Mehta Publishing House.

Datta, Sankar and Vipin Sharma (eds.) (2010). *State of India's Livelihoods: The 4P Report*. Access Development Services.

Datye, K.R. (1977). *Banking on Bio-mass: A New Strategy for Sustainable Prosperity Based on Renewable Energy and Dispersed Industrialisation*. Centre for Environment Education.

FAO (2011). *The State of Food and Agriculture 2010-2011-Women Closing the Gap*.

Glendenning, Claire J, Babu Suresh and Kwadwo Asenso-Okyere (2010). "Review of Agricultural Extension in India Are Farmers' Information Needs Being Met?", *IFPRI Discussion Paper* 01048, December. Eastern and Southern Africa Regional Office.

IFAD (2011). *Poverty Report, 2001*.

Krishna, A. and D. Bajpai (2011). "Lineal Spread and Radial Dissipation: Experiencing Growth in Rural India, 1993-2005", *Economic & Political Weekly* XLVI(38): 44-51, September 17.

Mahila Kisan Sashaktikaran Pariyojana (MKSP) 2011. *http://rural.nic.in/sites/programmes-schemes.asp*.

Ministry of Panchayati Raj. *http://panchayat.gov.in/mopr/viewPortalPage.do?cToken=-582425646*.

Ministry of Rural Development (2008). *Report of the Task Force on Convergence*. Developed by the Ministry of Rural Development around MGNREGA (GoI/MoRD).

NCAER (2008). *Perception Survey by the National Council of Applied Economic Research*.

NCEUS (2009). *The Challenge of Employment in India*. Vol. 1. National Commission on Enterprises in the Unorganised Sector. p.247.

NSSO (2005). *Situation Assessment Survey of Farmers: Access to Modern Technology for Farming*, 59th round (January–December 2003). Report No. 499(59/33/2). New Delhi: Ministry of Statistics and Programme Implementation.

Papola, T.S. (2010). "Livelihoods in Agriculture: Status, Policies and Prospects", in Sankar Datta and Vipin Sharma (eds.), *State of India's Livelihoods: The 4P Report*. Access Development Services.

Planning Commission (1998). *Tenth Five Year Plan*. Government of India.

————. (2007). *Working Group on Gender Issues, Panchayati Raj Institutions, Public Private Partnership, Innovative Finance and Micro-finance in Agriculture for the Eleventh Five Year Plan (2007-2012).* Government of India.

————. (2011). *Approach Paper to the Twelfth Five Year Plan*. Government of India.

Rajasthan Directorate of Economics and Statistics. *http://statistics.rajasthan.gov.in/socio_economic.htm*.

Rasheed, Sulaiman (2000). *Agricultural Extension in India-The Next Step*. New Delhi: National Centre for Agricultural Economics and Policy Research. January.

Singh, Harsh (2010). *Creating Vibrant Public-Private-Panchayat Partnership (PPPP) for Inclusive Growth through Inclusive Governance*. New Delhi: Academic Foundation.

————. (2012). *Structural Innovation for Inclusive Development in Bihar: The Navodaya Shahar Model.* New Delhi: Academic Foundation.

UN Solution Exchange (2011a) *For the Decentralization Community, Consolidated Reply-Query: Implementing MP Public Services Guarantee Act: Experiences; Referrals.* November 29th.

————. (2011b). For the UN Food and Nutrition Community of Practice.

World Bank (2010). *Synthesis Report*. Volume I (*http://www.nird.org.in/brgf/reports.html*)>

World Bank and the Organization for Economic Cooperation and Development (OECD), (2008). *Equality for Women: Where Do We Stand on Millennium Development Goal 3?*